Carlo Pedretti

LEONARDO
THE MACHINES

Note

Leonardo's manuscripts and drawings, all available in the Italian National Edition (Giunti), are cited according to customary usage, as follows:

CA	Codex Atlanticus in the Biblioteca Ambrosiana, Milan
Windsor RL	Anatomical manuscripts and drawings in the Royal Library, Windsor Castle
Codex Arundel	Arundel Codex 263 in the British Library, London (the former Library of the British Museum)
Forster Mss. I-III	Notebooks in the Library of the Victoria and Albert Museum, London
Madrid Mss. I and II	Codices in the Madrid Biblioteca Nacional
Mss. A-M	Codices and notebooks in the Library of the Institut de France, Paris
Codex Hammer	Manuscript (former Codex Leicester) owned by Bill Gates, Seattle, Washington (USA)
Codex Trivulzianus	Manuscript in the Biblioteca Trivulziana in Castello Sforzesco, Milan
Codex on the Flight of Birds	Manuscript in the Biblioteca Reale, Turin

The chronology of Leonardo's notes and drawings frequently varies even within the context of a single manuscript. Accordingly, for each image reproduced, the approximate or certain date is given.

Managing editor
Claudio Pescio

Graphics
Carlo Savona

Consultation graphics and pagination
Energia di Emanuela Crivellaro

Cover design
Fabio Filippi

Translation
Catherine Frost

ISBN 88-09-01469-3

Reprint	Year
10 9 8 7 6 5	2007 2006 2005 2004

Printed by Giunti Industrie Grafiche S.p.A. Prato

CONTENTS

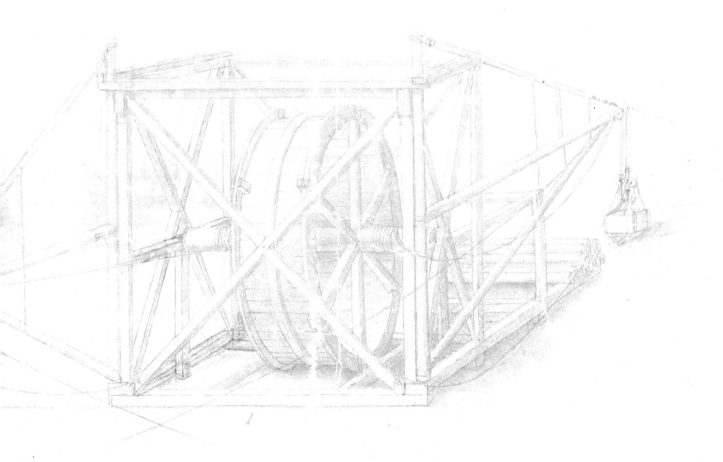

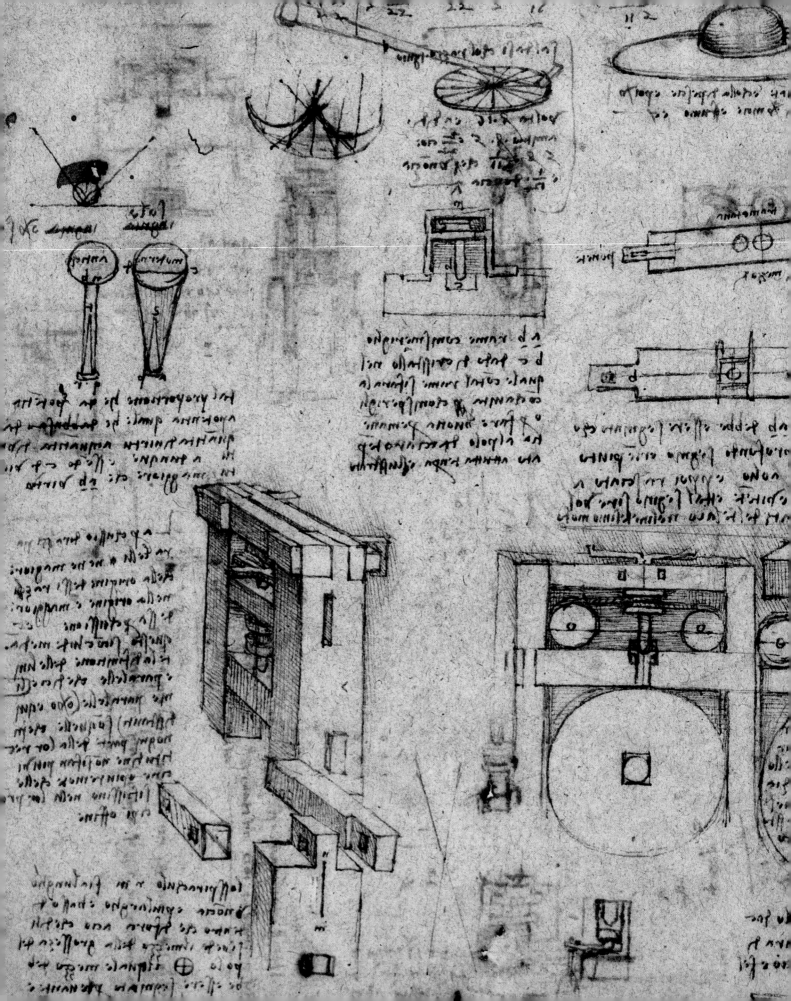

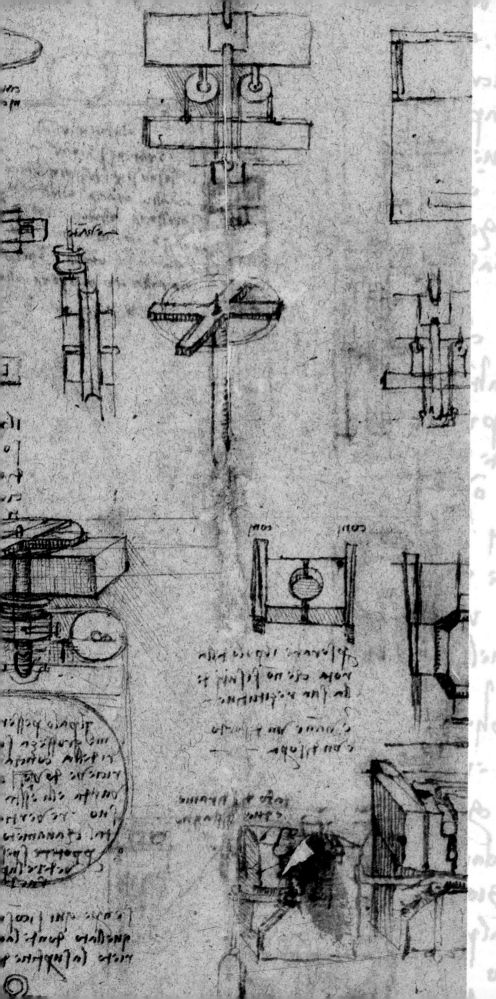

«True science»

The distinguishing trait of Leonardo the inventor, acknowledged by his contemporaries to be endowed with «archimedean ingenuity», was the strict scientific basis he deemed indispensable to any technological concept. Accordingly, he turned back to the Scholastic tradition to confer on the practical activity of the workshop the professional dignity accorded architects and engineers in antiquity. Throughout his extraordinary career as technologist, the striking example of Archimedes was always before him. With «true science» he conceived of new uses for the burning mirrors invented by the legendary Syracusan, and this to exploit solar energy for industrial purposes and even for astronomical observation.

Overleaf, on the two
preceding pages:
studies of
mechanisms for
constructing great
parabolic mirrors
used for exploiting
solar energy
CA f. 1036 ii v
c. 1513-1515

1. Experiments
with artificial
wing
Ms B f. 88 v
c. 1487-1490

2. Study for
flying machine
(the so-called
"helicopter")
Ms B f. 83 v
c. 1487-1490

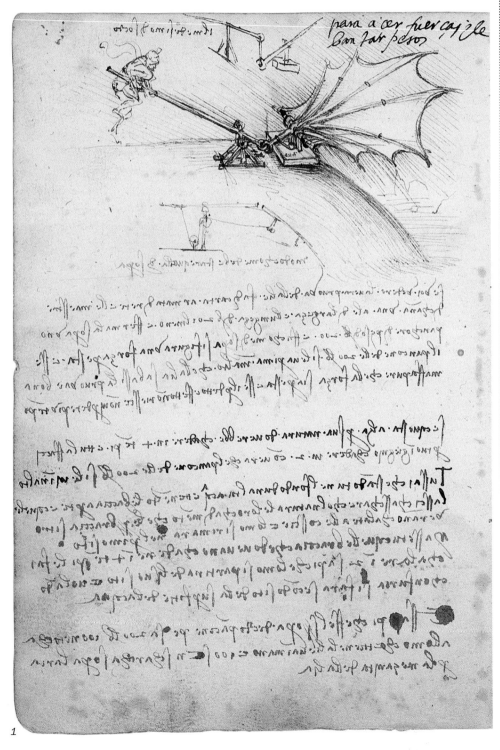

One day in the years between 1487 and 1490, Leonardo picked up a «thin wide ruler» that he was probably using to draw some geometric figure or machine component, and whirled it violently about in the air. Why we do not know. Perhaps he did it once by chance, and then again to verify a scientific theory that had flashed through his mind. He had suddenly realized that his arm tended to rise, guided by the motion of that blade whirling through the air. This is the basic principle of the helicopter – the helicopter of today, where the propeller is merely a double vane, and thus analogous to Leonardo's «thin wide ruler». Spinning that ruler, Leonardo realized that its angle of inclination caused it to rise through the air. And since his own shoulder was the fulcrum for the spinning, a spiral motion was created. In his mind, the whirling ruler became a continuous surface, like the helical thread on a screw: a surface swelling out like a sail which, instead of billowing in the wind, turned like a screw, «spiraling in the air and rising high».

From this to making an experimental model was only a short step. For Leonardo a sketch was sufficient, without entering into details but employing the structural elements of nautical technology: the great screw sail has its shrouds which provide stability, obviously rotating along with the hoops to which they are fixed. The motive force could only be a wound-up spring, like that of a clock, which can in fact be seen in the sketch beneath the axis of the aerial screw.

Although he does not say so, Leonardo was obviously thinking of the so-called "archimedean screw" that draws up water through a similar process. Moreover, water and air were for him similar elements, with the same conditions of cause and effect appearing in

1. Studies on flight
of birds
in relation
to the wind
Ms E f. 42 v
c. 1513-1514

2. Drawings of device
for rotating wing
Codex on the Flight
of Birds
ff. 16 v-17 r
c. 1505

3. Studies on flight
of birds
in relation
to the wind
Ms E f. 43 r
c. 1513-1514

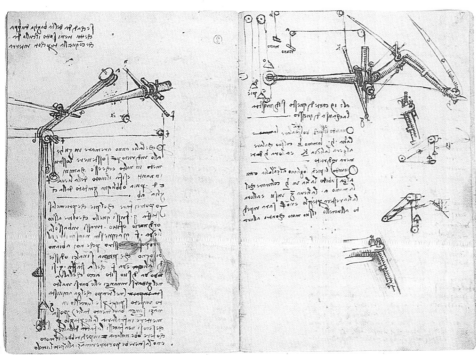

both. And so he studied the motion of fish to understand that of birds, and vice versa.

In 1513-1514 Leonardo, now sixty years old, finally formulated a theory of flight that could qualify as «true science», or «perceivable science», insofar as it could be perceived by the senses and could thus be verified by experiment.

«In order to give the true science of the movement of the birds in the air it is necessary first to give the science of the winds, and this we shall prove by means of the movements of the water. This science is in itself capable of being received by the senses: it will serve as a ladder to arrive at the perception of flying things in the air and the wind».

LEONARDO SCIENTIST?

With his renewed studies on the flight of birds, and in particular gliding flight assisted by the wind, Leonardo became increasingly convinced that man too could fly with the aid of a mechanical device. At that same time and in the same codex he wrote: «Mechanics is the paradise of the mathematical sciences, because by means of it one comes to the fruits of mathematics».

It may be said, paradoxically, that Leonardo arrived at the age of twenty-three without knowing the meaning of the word "science". Incredible as this may seem, it is the only explanation for the fact that, among the words he listed in about 1487 for which an explanation should be sought, as in a dictionary, are the following:

«Science: knowledge of the things that are possible present and past»; «Prescience: knowledge of the things which may come to pass».

This appears in the first manuscript compiled by Leonardo in Milan, the so-called Codex Trivulzianus, written

1. Studies on flight
   of birds
   Codex on the Flight
   of Birds
   f. 15 v
   c. 1505

2. Studies on flight
   of birds
   in relation to
   air currents
   Codex on the Flight
   of Birds
   f. 8 r
   c. 1505

slightly before the French Codex B, the one containing the study on the helicopter. The identification of "science" with "theory" (that is, the opposite of "practice"), according to a still-medieval concept, is confirmed by a note appearing several pages before: «Theoretical: science without practice». Moreover, Leonardo frequently uses the form "scientia" in place of "science", just as it appears in scholastic texts, always with the meaning of "theory"; «Ars sine scientia nihil est»: there can be no art, i.e., "practice", without theory, proclaimed the theoreticians who engineered the Duomo of Milan toward the end of the 14th century.

Accordingly, caution should be used in referring to Leonardo as a scientist, a term which in his days certainly did not have the same meaning as today. Those who studied the natural sciences – anatomy, zoology, botany, geology, meteorology and astronomy – were known as philosophers. As Vasari stated in regard to Leonardo's astronomical studies: «For which he formulated in his soul a concept so heretical that he embraced no religion of any kind, deeming it better to be a philosopher than a Christian».

This also explains the opinion expressed by Francis I, King of France, in 1542 in regard to Leonardo's scientific knowledge. As Cellini reports, «I feel that I must not neglet to repeat the exact words which I heard from the King's own lips about Crim, which he told me in the presence of the Cardinal of Ferrara, the Cardinal of Lorraine, and the King of Navarre. He said that he did not believe that there had ever been another man born into the world who had known as musch as Leonardo, and this not only in matters concerning Sculpture. Painting and Architecture, but because he was a very great Philosopher».

A philosopher was of course a ma-

1. Homo vitruvianus
   *from Cesare
   Cesariano's edition
   of* Vitruvius
   (Como 1521)

2. Homo vitruvianus
   *as a robot
   From the dust
   jacket of the book
   by Mark E.
   Rosheim,* Robot
   Wrist Actuators
   (New York 1989)

3. Homo vitruvianus
   *Venice,
   Accademia
   Galleries
   n. 228
   c. 1490*

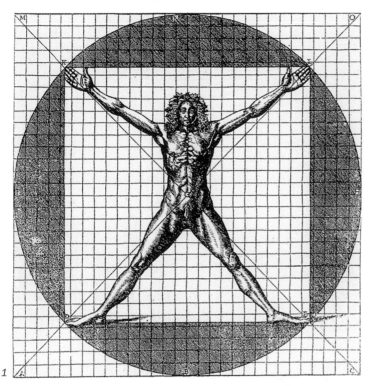

1

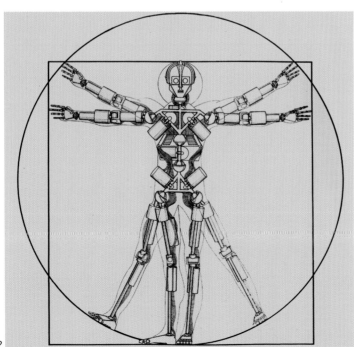

2

thematician as well, more specifically interested in arithmetic, geometry, stereometry, mechanics, statics, dynamics, optics, acoustics, and hydraulics. The geometer was already engaging in practical applications such as land-surveying, and could thus work beside the architect, to whom geometry (like other sciences) was necessary for designing buildings. Then came the cosmographer, who produced nautical and celestial charts.

THEORY AND PRACTICE

Leonardo as a child received the first rudiments of arithmetic and grammar at the "scuola dell'abbaco", or primary school, where he learned to read, write and do sums. After this he entered a workshop to learn art, that is, the practice of painting and sculpture. Within this context, architecture too might be involved. This activity, consisted mainly of producing a wooden model of an architect's project, still remained within the sphere of sculpture. But the step was brief and it was better to be prepared. A more thorough knowledge of geometry was needed, indispensable moreover for studying human proportions and perspective. And the architect himself, as exemplified by Vitruvius, must study proportion and optical techniques. Leonardo's famous drawing of a man inscribed in a circle and a square is actually an illustration – in fact, the first illustration, datable around 1490 – of the theories on proportion postulated by Vitruvius in the 1st century BC as basis for the study of architecture.

Painting and architecture, then, can and must proceed side by side, as Brunelleschi and Masaccio had already understood. And in fact the first renovator of Italian painting, Giotto, was also an architect. Giorgio Vasari tells us that Verrocchio himself, as a youth, had assiduously studied geome-

1. Detail of a painting by Biagio di Antonio, Tobias and the Archangels (c. 1470); Florence, Bartolini Salimbeni Collection, showing the lantern of the Florence Cathedral under construction.

2. Revolving crane CA f. 965 r c. 1478-1480

3. Model of revolving crane (1987) Florence, Museum of History of Science

4. Dome of the Florence Cathedral, detail of the lantern

1

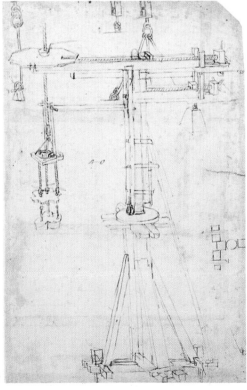

2

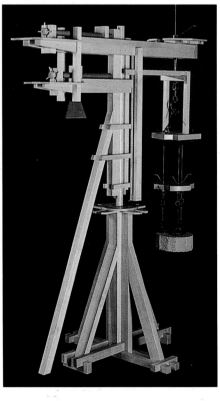

3

try. It is not surprising, then, that geometric figures already appear on Leonardo's earliest folios, from 1478 on, alongside the first drawings of machines, most of them reproductions of devices invented by Brunelleschi to be used in constructing the dome for the Florence Cathedral, around 1420.

This link with Brunelleschi's technological tradition is also explained by the fact that in 1469 Andrea del Verrocchio had been commissioned to construct a copper ball, two and a half meters in diameter, to be placed on top of the lantern on Brunelleschi's dome. It was to be the final touch to the greatest monument of the Florentine "Quattrocento", a symbol of the relationship between the arts: an abstract sculpture in the most perfect geometric shape, designed to crown a work of architecture. Its practical realization involved the technological problem of raising it to the top of the dome, a feat which was accomplished in the year 1470.

Leonard, who had recently entered Verrocchio's workshop, was able to observe the whole operation, and probably contributed to it as well. This was not merely an undertaking requiring manual skill and technical capability; it was also a project of scientific endeavor. For the first time Leonardo felt the fascination of calculation and geometry, an experience he was never to forget. In 1515, at the age of sixty-three, he was to write: «Remember the solderings which were used to solder the ball of Santa Maria del Fiore».

Forty-five years later; it was the time of his studies on harnessing solar energy through parabolic mirrors. This same system, whose origins date back to antiquity, had already been employed by Leonardo's master Verrocchio to weld together the numerous sections of the copper ball to be placed atop the dome of the Florence

1. Studies and
calculations on
parabolic mirrors
with note (f. 84 v)
on use of burning
mirrors in 1469
to solder the copper
ball for the lantern
on the Florence

Cathedral
Ms G ff. 84 v-85 r
c. 1515

2. Machines for
manufacturing
concave mirrors
CA f. 1103 v
c. 1503-1505

3.-4. Machines
for manufacturing
concave mirrors
Madrid Ms I
f. 61 r
c. 1495-1497
Ms B f. 13 r
c. 1487-1490

5. Devices for
manufacturing
concave mirrors
CA f. 17 v
c. 1478-1480

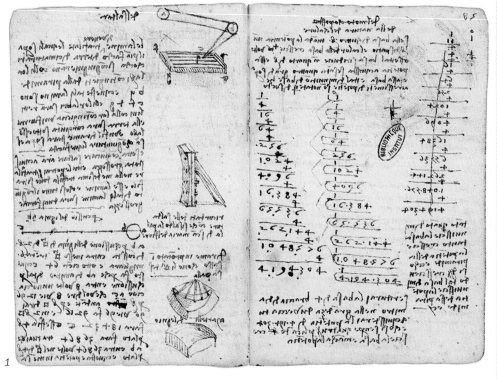

1

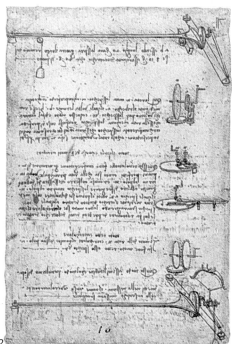

2

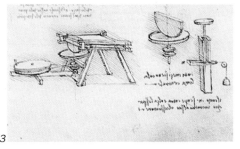

3

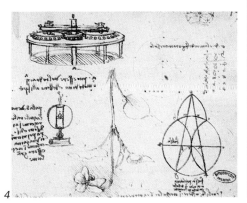

4

Cathedral. The curvature of the geometrically established sections had been scrupulously calculated in relation to what was to be the center of the ball. This could not be done by eye. Devices for controlling the shape assumed by the copper plates under the blows of the hammer had to be designed. And the shearing of the curvilinear sides had to be precise to the millimeter to achieve the final effect of a continuous surface, smooth and gilded, perfectly reflecting the sun's rays.

OPTICS AND ENERGY

The equipment used for welding had to be perfected too. The oxyhydrogen flame had not yet been invented, and small welds were executed at the forge. For large ones instead greater power was required, and the only source available was the sun. For this purpose catoptrics, the science of mirrors, was necessary. It could be learned from the classical texts of Ptolemy, Euclid and Archimedes, and from Medieval compendiums such as those of Vitellius and Alhazen, to which Lorenzo Ghiberti had also referred for his *Commentaries* published in 1450.

This explains the insistence with which Leonardo, in his early folios, studied machines that could be used to produce burning mirrors, or «fire mirrors» as he called them. Ranging in diameter from seventy centimeters to one meter, they could be manufactured in a single piece. Their curvature was of course calculated according to the point at which the reflected rays would be concentrated, where smelting was to take place. It was thus a question of determining what scientists today call the "caustic of reflection" or "catacaustic".

Only a few traces of these calculations are found in the young Leonar-

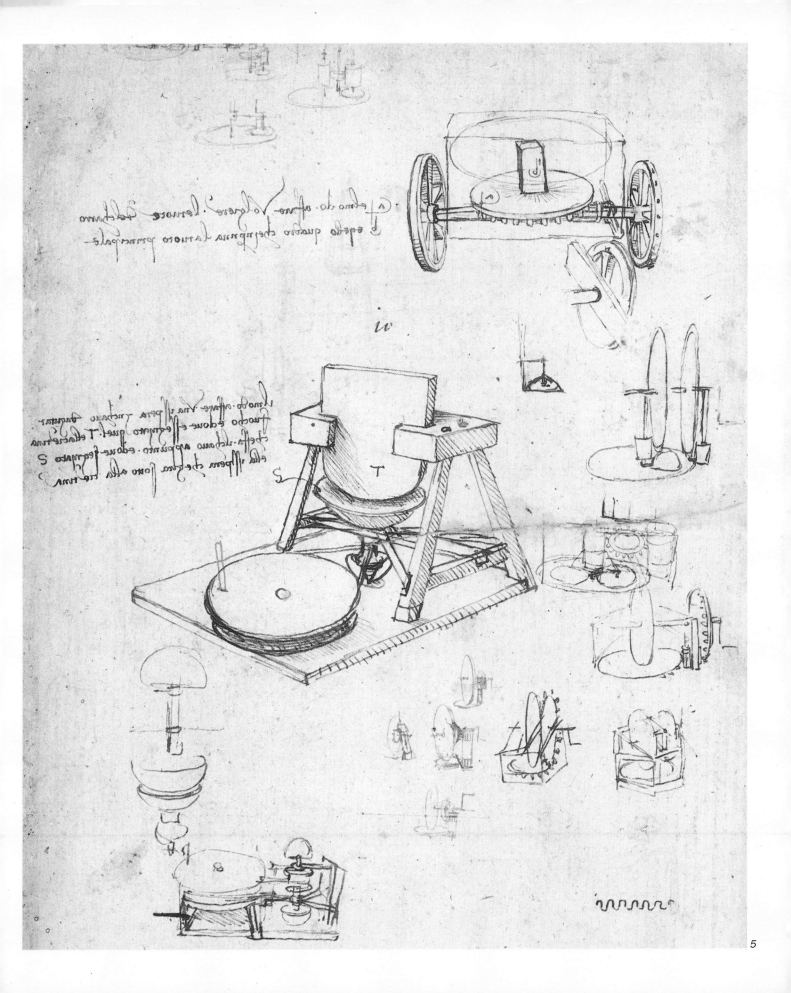

5

1. Studies on reflection caustics and device for manufacturing parabolic mirrors CA f. 823 i r c. 1503-1505

2. Studies of large parabolic mirrors for exploiting solar energy CA f. 750 r c. 1513-1515

3. Studies on reflection caustics and device for manufacturing parabolic mirrors Codex Arundel ff. 86 v-87 r c. 1503-1505

4. Studies on reflection caustics and device for manufacturing parabolic mirrors Codex Arundel ff. 84 v-88r c. 1503-1505

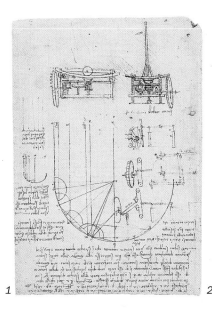

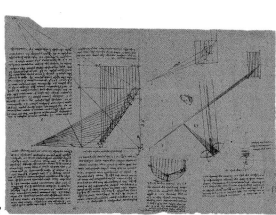

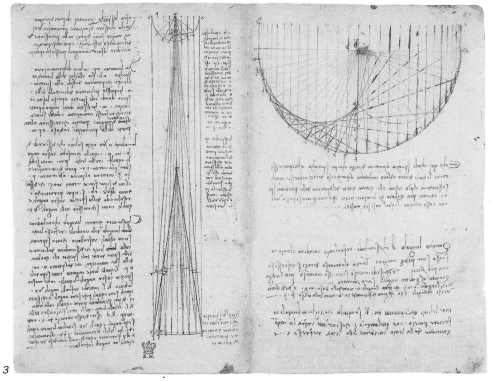

do's papers. Later, after 1500, they are instead abundant, and accompanied by stupendous geometric drawings. We will now try to understand why.

Machines used to produce mirrors, perfected in comparison to those appearing in the early folios, frequently recur in Leonardo's manuscripts from the last years of the 15th century on. The mirrors were mostly of normal diameter. But around 1503-05, the idea of a burning mirror of great size, like those used by Archimedes to set fire to the Roman ships at Syracuse, began to emerge. This could also explain why, in one of the first published mentions of Leonard, in the *De sculptura* by his contemporary theoretician Luca Gaurico in 1504, the artist is cited not only as a pupil of Verrocchio but also as being endowed with «archimedean ingenuity». Producing a concave mirror surface like that of the great antennas of today's space probes was practically impossible in those days. But remembering the great ball that Verrocchio had built in sections, Leonardo realized that the same system could be applied to constructing a parabolic mirror. A very high-precision instrument would however be needed, a "templet" to smooth the various sections to the established curvature.

1513-1516: Leonardo was in Rome, working in the Vatican for Giuliano de' Medici, the Pope's brother. Two German technicians, mirror manufacturers, were his assistants. Project: installing equipment to exploit solar energy for industrial use. It seems that the Medici intended to develop a textile industry in Rome like the one that had brought prosperity to Florence.

Leonardo's studies barely hint at the purpose of the project: «One wonders whether the "pyramid" [the pyramid is the bundle of reflected solar rays] can be condensed to bring so much power to one single point and whether it ac-

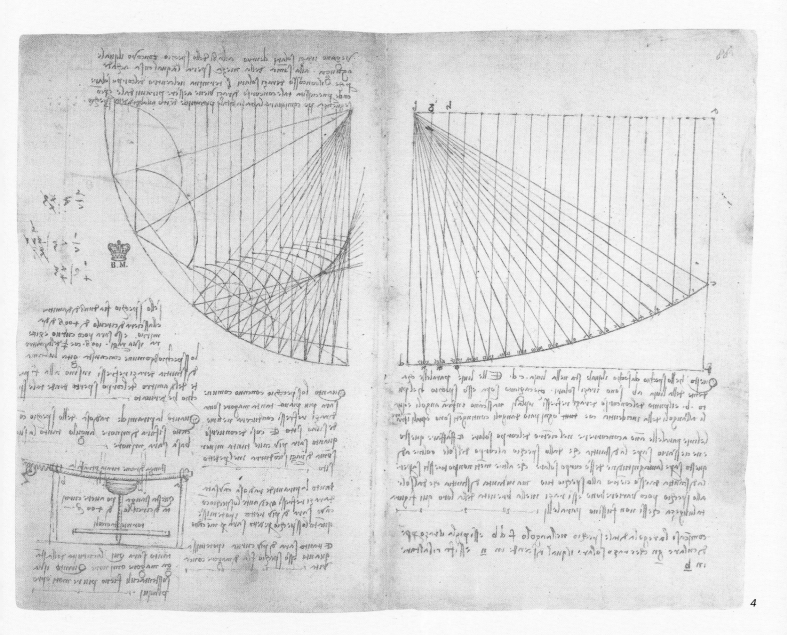

1. Anatomical
   studies
   of eyeballs
   Windsor RL
   12602 r
   c. 1506-1508

2. Studies on
   proportions
   of the face
   with detail
   of eyes
   Turin,
   Biblioteca Reale
   no. 15574
   c. 1490

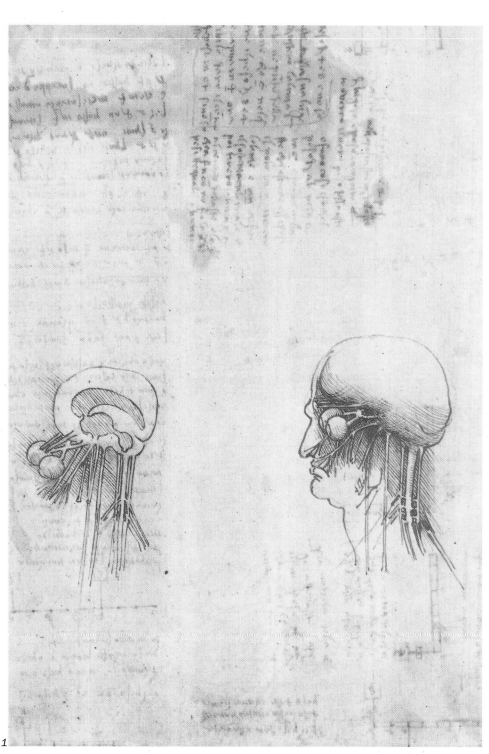

1

quires more density than the air that sustains it». And then, immediately afterward, the note that reveals what it is all about: «With this one can supply heat for any boiler in a dyeing factory. And with this a pool can be warmed up, because there will be always boiling water». So it was a system of central heating that could also be used to heat swimming pools. But this was not all. The enormous burning mirror constructed in sections is actually a multi-block telescope.

ASTRONOMICAL OBSERVATION

On a page of calculations and diagrams for this project appear the words: «To observe the nature of the planets have an opening made in the roof and show at the base one planet singly: the reflected movement on this base will record the structure of the said planet, but arrange so that this base only reflects one at a time».

Although it is certain that Leonardo was suggesting using the parabolic mirror for astronomical observations, the note merely gives an idea of the procedure without furnishing details, and as such it may appear incomprehensible. Leonardo does say however to open the roof, just as in an astronomical observatory. To show a planet at the «base» means directing the mirror so as to receive the planet in the base of the reflection pyramid. The «reflected motion of said base» is thus the reflection at the focal point, where the «structure ("complessione") of the planet», magnified, can be observed. The «complessione» is the surface, like that of the skin. The «base», concludes Leonardo, should center one planet at a time. This is no less than an allusion to Newton's reflecting telescope, although it is not explained how the enlarged image of the planet will be transmitted to the observer. Perhaps the telescope was only an idea.

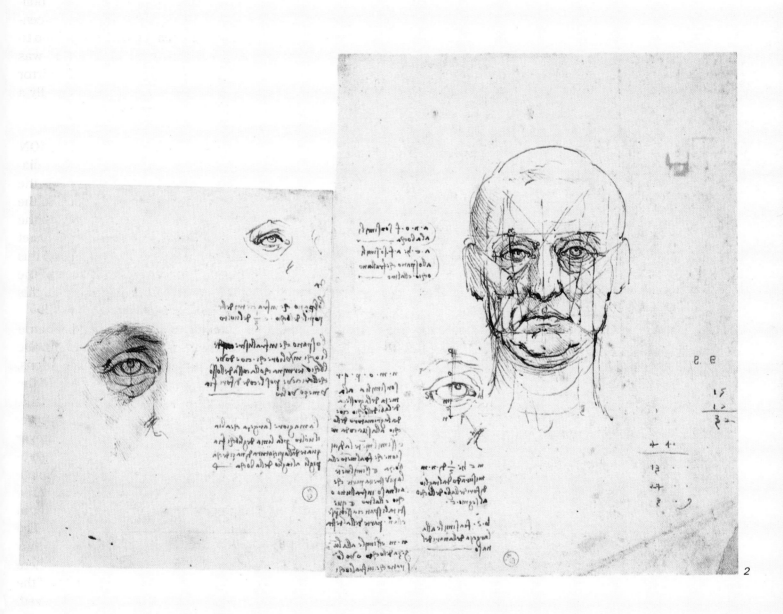

2

1. Demonstration of mechanism of the eye using glass model Ms D f. 3 v c. 1508

2. Study of astronomy with explanation of the «earth-shine» of the new moon (one hundred years before Galileo) Codex Hammer f. 2 r c. 1508

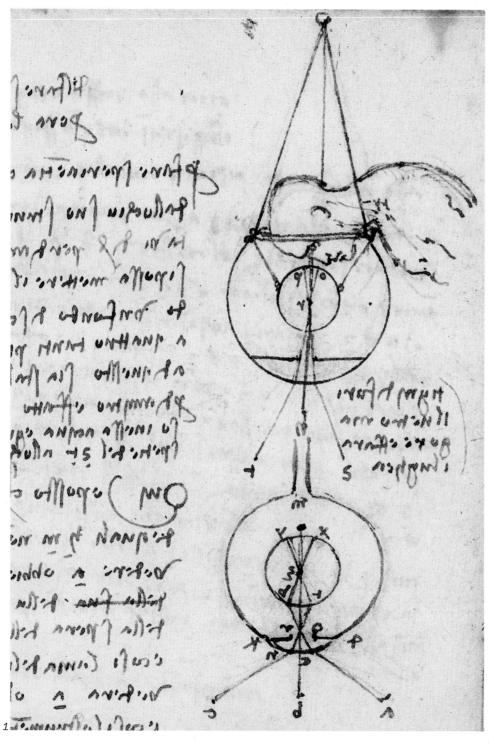

Otherwise Leonardo would have realized that there is no water on the moon, contrary to his belief. And yet, in the experimental stage, he must have constructed some device for astronomical observation, although without achieving the results attained by Galileo a century later. «Make lenses to see the moon large». And still further: «If you keep the details of the spots on the moon under observation you will often find great differences in them, and I have myself proved this by making drawings of them».

The multi-block telescope, like so many other projects, was to end in nothing. «Barely begun, it was drowned: by the circumstances», reads a note on a sheet from that period. Leonardo's German assistants went into business for themselves in the Vatican, manufacturing mirrors to be sold at fairs. Leonardo, deeply perturbed, suffered a first breakdown.

Yet some knowledge of his ideas and scientific projects from that period, entrusted to his notes and even to scale drawings, all now lost, must have become known from his manuscripts after his death. The suspicion arises from this comment made by the philosopher Arrigo Cornelio Agrippa in his *Della vanità delle scienze* (Venice 1552): «And I know how to make mirrors in which all the things illuminated by the shining Sun, and regardless of their distance, whether it is four or five miles, can be seen most clearly».

When Leonardo moved to Milan in 1482 he found greater scope for dedicating himself to scientific studies, since his activity in that city was focused mainly on civil and military engineering and technology. The architectural projects he was involved in from 1487 to 1490, in particular that of the "tiburio", or central tower of the Milan Cathedral, led him to study the principles of statics inherent to the thrust of

1. *Study of thrust on arches for the lantern of the Milan Cathedral CA f. 850 r c. 1487-1490*

2.-5. *Studies on statics and dynamics of arches Madrid Ms I f. 143 r c. 1495 Ms A ff. 49 and 53 r c. 1492 Madrid Ms I f. 139 r c. 1495*

6. *First ideas for the lantern on the Milan Cathedral on a folio of studies of figures, caricature profiles and studies of hydraulic wheel CA f. 719 r c. 1487*

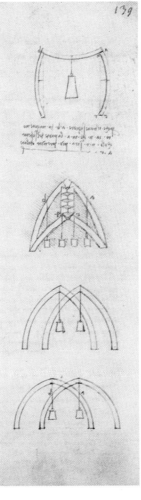

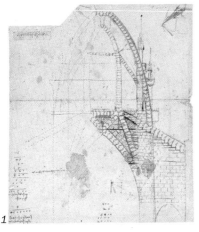

arches. And the projects for weapons are related to studies on mechanics concerning theories of striking, impetus, rebound and inertia, conducted in the early 1490s.

SCIENTIFIC ILLUSTRATION

At the same time Leonardo began his studies on water, which gave rise to his interest in hydraulics and hydrostatics, just as painting had stimulated his interest in optics and anatomy. Soon these active scientific interests were to intermingle in an intense program of interdisciplinary research. Leonardo now had to report the results of his observations in manuscripts to which he could constantly refer, in a continuous process of elaboration and reviewing, all effectively presented through the immediacy of visual language.

Leonardo's enormous contribution to the scientific writings of the Sixteenth Century was, in fact, this: the use of illustration. It can be evaluated in the later treatises on architecture and anatomy such as those of Sebastiano Serlio and Andrea Vesalio, not to mention the books on machines by authors ranging from Giovanni Branca to Agostino Ramelli, or the monumental work of Ulisse Aldrovandi on the natural sciences. Leonardo himself, in his anatomical studies of 1510, acknowledges to drawing the faculty of providing «true information» on the limbs and their functions, «and in this way you will give the true conception of their shapes, which neither ancient nor modern writers have ever been able to give without an infinitely tedious and confused prolixity of writing and of time».

Unfortunately, what has remained of Leonardo's writings is not sufficient to allow objective evaluation of his contribution to the «theoretical». The mathematician Luca Pacioli, a

1. 3. Studies for a
repertoire of
«mechanical
elements»
Ms I Madrid
ff. 8 v, 9 v, 10 r
c. 1495-1497

2. Studies for a
manually
operated
elevator device
Ms I Madrid
f. 9 r
c. 1495-1497

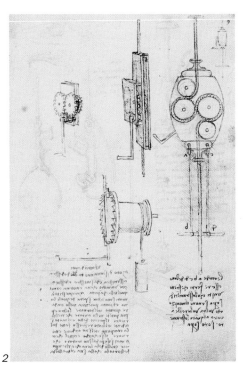

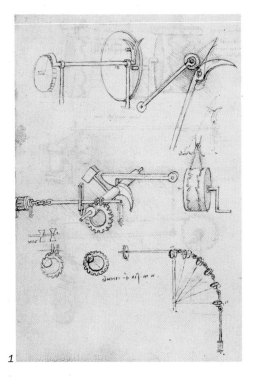

1

2

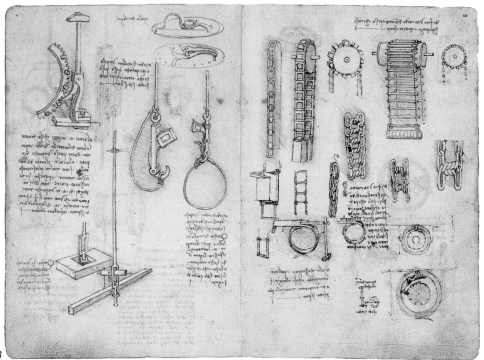

3

treatise writer by profession, mentions one of Leonardo's treatises, *Del moto locale et de le forze tutte, cioè pesi accidentali,* in a work dated 1498.

It is thus unjust to belittle Leonardo's scientific contribution, which was moreover acknowledged by contemporaries such as the mathematician Pacioli, the physician and historian Paolo Giovio and the philosopher Gerolamo Cardano, on the grounds that he lacked the formal and academic training, and even the temperament, of the treatise writer. Luckily, it can now be stated, instead of knowing Latin as his father did; he knew how to draw.

The Milanese art historian Giovan Paolo Lomazzo expressed a different opinion in 1590, after having seen Leonardo's books still integral at the home of Francesco Melzi, his pupil and heir. After having mentioned those on human and equine anatomy, on proportions and perspective, he notes the existence of «many other books, in which he showed how many movements and aspects can be explained by mathematical principles». And adds, «And he showed the art of pulling weights, and this in books of which the whole of Europe is full, and which the experts keep in highest esteem, judging that nothing more can be done that what he did».

The wide-spread diffusion of Leonardo's scientific ideas implied by Lomazzo, noticeable especially in Germany and Flanders, has been confirmed by recent research, that of the Leonardo scholar Ladislao Reti in particular, responsible among other things for the critical edition of the Madrid manuscripts found in the 1960s, the first of which is a true repertoire of «mechanical elements», i.e., those which carry out a primary function in the structure and operation of each machine.

Since it was presented for the first time by Gilberto Govi in a brief communication to the Academy of Sciences in Paris (*Sur une très ancienne application de l'hélice comme organe de propulsion*) in 1881, Leonardo's small drawing on f. 83 v of Codex B of the Institut de France has been the subject of repeated interpretations and comments which have led to its reconstruction in models (frequently arbitrary) for Leonardo museums or itinerant exhibitions. Suitable updating, also bibliographic, of the pertinent technological problems discussed in my *Studi vinciani* of 1957 (pp. 125-129) can be found in the essay by Giovanni P. Galdi, *Leonardo's Helicopter and Archimedes Screw: The Principle of Action and Reaction*, in

THE HELICOPTER
AND THE HANG GLIDER

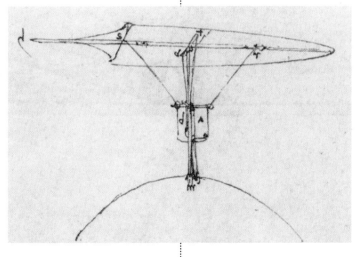

Above, the "helicopter" in Ms B f. 83 v c. 1487-1490 Left, model of Leonardo's helicopter, Milan, Museum of Science and Technology

Below, studies of kites for sailplaning flight Madrid Ms I, f. 64 r c. 1497 Right, model of Leonardo's "hang glider", constructed in Great Britain in 1993

first decade of Leonardo's stay in Milan, from 1482 to 1490, the idea of an ornithopter, a machine designed to reproduce the beating wings of birds, predominates. Around 1505 Leonardo realized that the best solution would be a machine for gliding flight maneuvered by the pilot who could change its center of gravity by simply shifting the position of the upper part of his body.

This is the principle of the hang glider, at which Leonardo arrived not only through systematic study of the flight of birds but also by observing the behavior of kites, some of the largest of which were capable of lifting a man off the ground. This is explained on f. 64 r of the Madrid Ms I, where such a device is actually designed in a

"Achademia Leonardi Vinci", IV, 1991, pp. 193-195. Precedents, even from medieval times, have been found in miniatures showing children playing with toys of a kind still in use in modern times, consisting of a threaded rod along which a rising thrust is imparted to a bladed device that whirls off it into the air. Cf. Ladislao Reti, *Helicopters and Whirligigs*, in "Raccolta Vinciana", XX, 1964, pp. 331-338, with reference to previous publications on the same subject by Charles H. Gibbs-Smith.

However, the best comment on Leonardo's drawing is still his own text which accompanies it: «Let the outer extremity of the screw be of steel wire as thick as a cord, and from the circumference to the cen-

tre let it be "braccia" [approximately 5 meters]. I find that if this instrument made with a screw be well made – that is to say made of linen of which the pores are stopped up with starch – and be turned swiftly, the said will make its spiral in the air and it will rise high. Take the example of a wide and thin ruler whirled very rapidly in the air, and you will see that your arm will be guided by the line of the edge of the said flat surface. The framework of the above-mentioned linen should be of long stout cane. You

may make a small model of pasteboard, of which the axis is formed of fine steel wire, bent by force, and as it is released it will turn the screw».

The vast "corpus" of Leonardo's studies on flight was enriched in the 1960s by the discovery of two of his manuscripts in Madrid. The second of these, written in around 1504, contains notes on the flight of birds, while drawings of flying machines appear on a folio from the first, datable to about 1497. In the manuscripts dating back to the

spherical shape to sail on the wind down a mountain slope, while «the man will remain standing» in Cardan's suspension in a spherical cage at its center.

The other device appearing on the same page already shows all of the characteristics of the hang glider. A model of it was constructed for the first time in 1993, and attempts at flight were made in England (see "Achademia Leonardi Vinci", VI, 1993, pp. 222-225), while a version more faithful to Leonardo's drawing has recently been built at Sigillo in Umbria by the local association "Progetto Insieme" with the consultation of Alessandro Vezzosi, within the context of the educational-exhibition activities of the Museo Ideale at Vinci.

The tools of knowledge

The extraordinary combination of art, science and technology that marked Leonardo's fervent theoretical and practical activity in every field of knowledge can be explained by the historical and cultural context surrounding him in Florence and Milan during the latter half of the Fifteenth Century. His manuscripts bear witness to the serious intent with which he carried out an arduous program of study, referring to traditional sources, ancient and medieval, also through the mediation of contemporary experts such as the mathematician Luca Pacioli. In the early years of the Sixteenth Century Leonardo, by now «most impatient with his brush», was wholly absorbed in the fervor of scientific research.

Overleaf, on the two
preceding pages:
first studies
for sailplaning
flight
CA f. 70 ii r
c. 1493-1495

1. *Lorenzo de' Medici
in a sketch
by Leonardo
Windsor RL 12442 r
(from CA f. 902 ii r)
c. 1483-1485*

2. *Ludovico il Moro
in a detail from the
Pala Sforzesca by*

*an anonymous
Lombard painter of
the late 15th century
Milan, Brera*

3. *Architectural
studies for the
cathedral of Pavia
CA f. 362 v-b
c. 1487-1490*

4. *Studies of churches
with circular plan,
of reverberatory
furnaces and of a
«tool with spheres»
used in
manufacturing
burning mirrors
Ms B f. 21 v
c. 1487-1490*

1

2

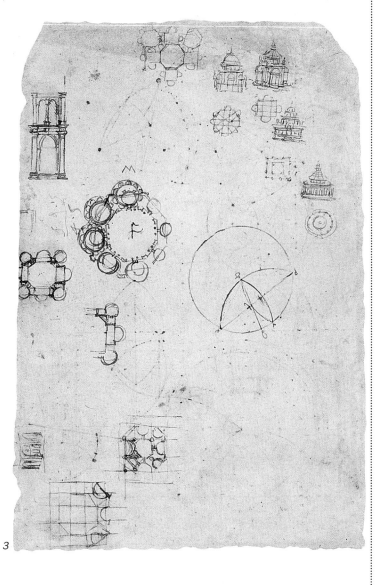

3

The culture linked to the universities in the great cities of Northern Italy, from Milan to Pavia, and Padua in particular, was different from that of Lorenzo de' Medici's Florence. Leonardo realized this as soon as he arrived in Milan in 1482. Although unable to evaluate the underlying reasons, he could not fail to realize that in his homeland, Florence, the emphasis was placed on those aspects of moral philosophy which concur to define the civic stature of man.

The philosopher Marsilio Ficino had in fact established, at the desire of Lorenzo himself, the Neo-Platonic Academy which in studying and interpreting the works of Plato sought to define a social order based on man's dignity and spiritual uplifting.

SCIENCE AND CULTURE IN MILAN

Milan was instead more pragmatic, as could be seen at a glance in the vast plains crisscrossed by a great network of canals planned by Francesco Sforza to stimulate industry as well as agriculture and commerce. University teaching was focused on study of the physical world, of nature. It was the teaching of Aristotle's natural philosophy that had been renewed in the famous schools of Oxford and Paris and that had spread over Northern Italy already in Medieval times. In Milan, Leonardo soon came into contact with the eminent personages of scientific culture. The occasion was offered him by Ludovico Sforza, who encouraged the arts and even organized meetings and scientific debates among the learned, including professors from the Pavia; and for once Leonardo too was included.

Scientific education in Milan and Pavia was often a family profession, as in the case of the Marliani. The distinguished writings, both published and unpublished, of the recently deceased

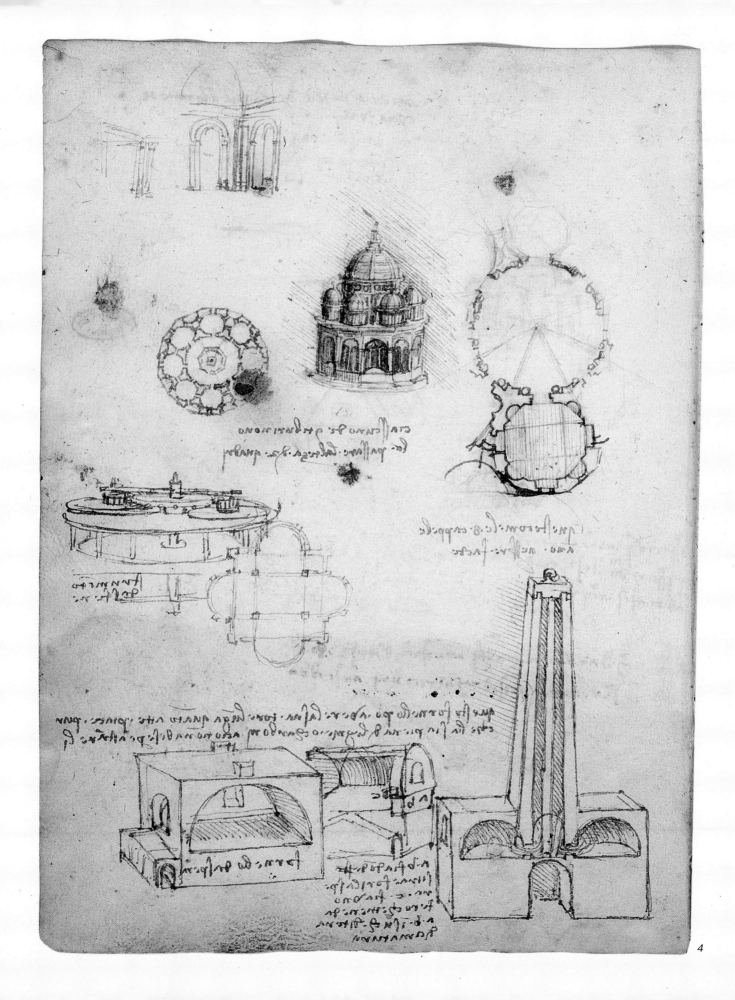

4

1. Study of church
   with circular
   plan
   Ms B f. 95 r
   (Ashburnham
   Ms f. 5 r)
   c. 1487-1490

2. Wooden model
   of building shown
   in the preceding
   figure
   Florence,
   Museum of History
   of Science
   1987

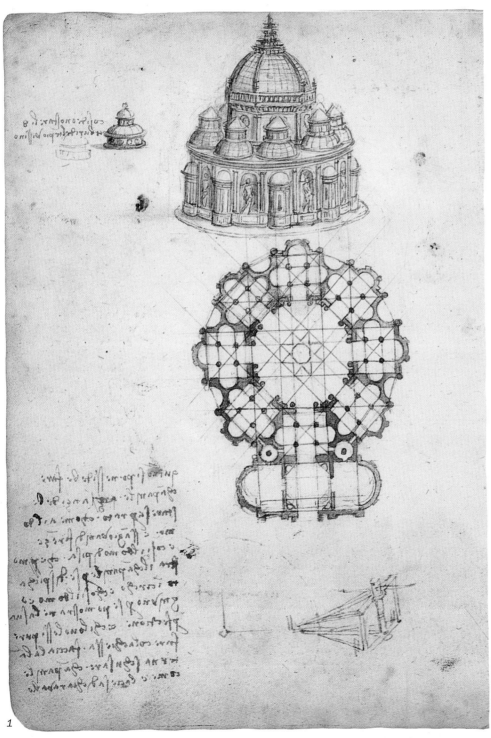

1

physician and mathematician Giovanni Marliani induced Leonardo to meet his sons, Gerolamo and Pier Antonio, who were also learned in the mathematical science: «Algebra, which the Marliani have, made by their father». In particular, Leonardo was interested in Marliani's observations on the relationship between light and shadow, a problem with which he himself was intensely concerned in about 1490. Although Marliani's works were all in Latin, Leonardo was able to understand them, perhaps with the help of a friend who translated or explained them. He could thus discuss them, at least with himself: «How can one have certain dense bodies that do not cast any shadow on their juxtaposed object. The Marliani science [i.e., theory] is therefore false».

In approaching the texts of ancient and Medieval knowledge, Leonardo recurred to experimental verification and contributed to the renewal of science by establishing mathematical justification as criterion for rationality. He could thus state: «There is no certainty where one can neither apply any of the mathematical sciences nor any of those which are based upon mathematical sciences». Observation and experience were thus the prerequisites for the formulation of physical laws: «It is my intention first to cite experience, then to show by reasoning why this experience is constrained to act in this manner. And this is the rule according to which speculators as to natural effects have to proceed».

From this came a break with tradition and his definition of «true science», that which goes beyond conceptual analysis: «No human investigation can be termed true science if it is not capable of mathematical demonstration. If you say that the sciences which begin and end in the mind are true, this is not conceded, but is de-

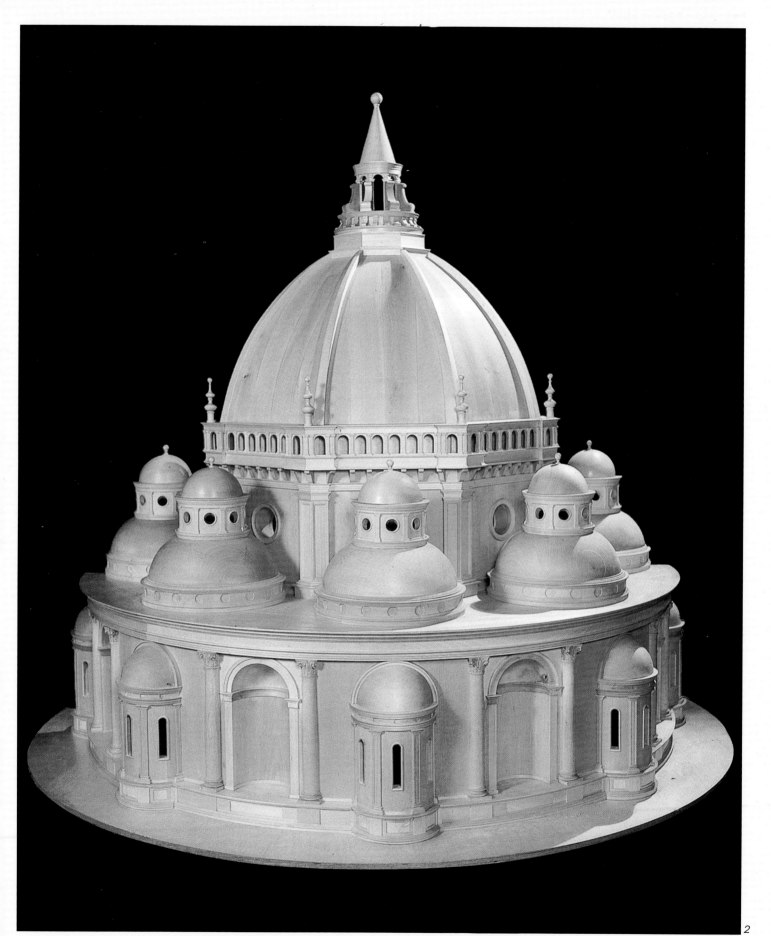

1-4. Principles
of proportion and
center of gravity
in studies of skull
dated by Leonardo
himself
«2 April 1489»
Windsor RL
19057 r, 19057 v,
19058 r, 19058 v

5. «Body born of
the perspective
of Leonardo
da Vinci, disciple
of experience»
CA f. 520 r
c. 1490

nied for many reasons, and foremost among these is the fact that the test of experience is absent from these exercises of the mind, and without these there is no assurance of certainty».

This is a text known only through a copy in the first chapter of the *Libro di pittura* (compiled after Leonardo's death), in which he proposes to demonstrate that painting is science. In a manuscript from 1515 he repeats the same concepts: «There is no certainty where one can neither apply any of the mathematical sciences nor any of those which are based upon the mathematical sciences».

THE BASIS OF KNOWLEDGE

All this began in the early days of Leonardo's stay in Milan. The meetings and confrontations were not always serene and cordial. «They will say that because of my lack of book-learning, I cannot properly express what I desire to treat of». This explains that geometric drawing of a body executed at the very time this statement was made, around 1490, under which appear the words: «Body born of the perspective of Leonardo Vinci, disciple of experience». This is followed by an explanation of what is involved: «Let this body be made without any relation to anybody, but out of simple lines only».

Perspective, proportion and mechanics. These are the cornerstones of the scientific basis of the study of art, and to them Leonardo turned from the very beginning of his stay in Milan. The Classical and Medieval texts he studied were subjected to the verification of experience through mathematical calculation. In the Medieval *Treatise of Proportions* by the Arab Al Kindi, a work particularly well-known in the Milan of the 15th century, Leonardo could find a note of agreement, since the author had proclaimed that «it is impossible to understand philosophy

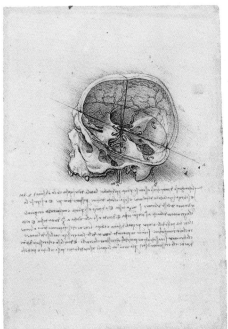

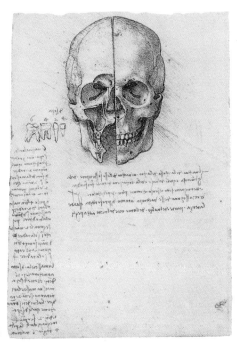

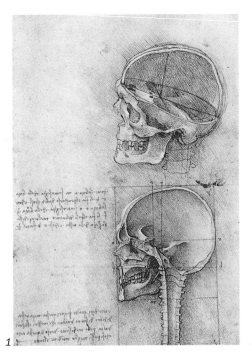

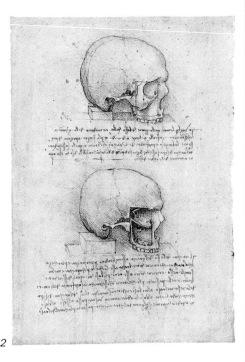

1

2

3

4

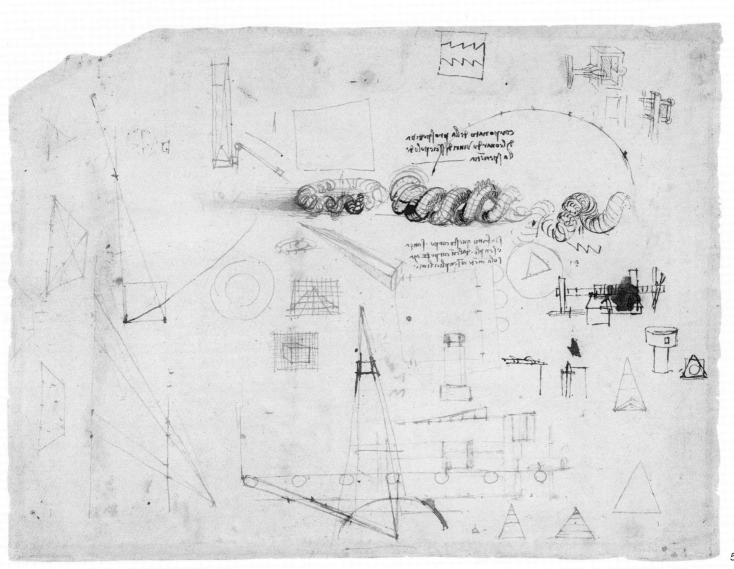

5

1. Illustration for De divina proportione by Luca Pacioli (1498): panel with the "Duodecedron elevatus vacuus"

2.-3. Solid geometry and polyhedrons Ms E f. 56 r c. 1513-1514 Forster Ms I f. 5 r 1505

4. Detail of sketch of a dodecahedron on a folio of studies of fortifications CA f. 942 v c. 1503-1504

5. Illustration of the geometric principles of proportions applied to architecture on a folio of anatomical studies Windsor RL 12608 r c. 1485-1487

1

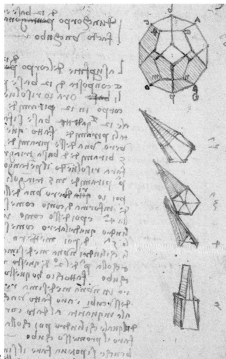
2

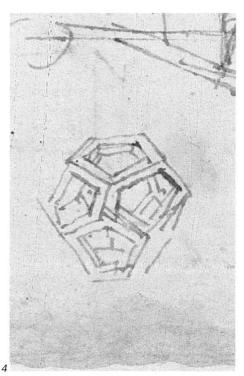
3

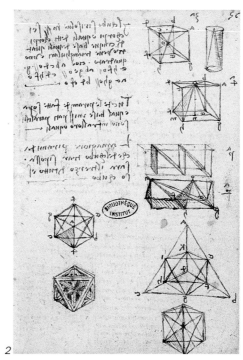
4

without a knowledge of mathematics». Leonardo was acquainted with this work through the version with comments by Giovanni Marliani given him by the physician Fazio Cardano, father of the great philosopher Gerolamo: «Alchendi's proportions as explained by Marliani: Messer Fazio has it». Fazio Cardano had, among other things, published the *Prospettiva communis* by the philosopher Giovanni Peckham, from which Leonardo was to take the famous eulogy to light translated into Italian. For Leonardo, what was proportion? He tells us in a note from 1505: «Proportion is found not only in numbers and measurements but also in sounds, weights, time, positions, and in whatsoever power there may be».

This explains Leonard's anthropometric interests in about 1490, which ranged from graphic interpretation of Vitruvius' principles to minute measurements performed on the human body through an analytic-comparative method, correlating for example the height of the head to that of the foot and other limbs.

THE STUDY OF GEOMETRY

Leonardo's first anatomical studies were, in fact, based on proportional schemes used to determine the factors of weight and balance in the human body. The famous Windsor drawings of skulls, dated 1489 by Leonardo himself, illustrate how these schemes were used to identify the center of gravity in a cross-section view of the skull, as in a geometric body.

Leonardo, as we know, had studied geometry already as a young man in Florence. In Milan he resumed these studies immediately, along with those of painting, anatomy, optics, mechanics and hydraulics. Geometry was for him the foundation stone of all aspects of scientific research and interpreta-

5

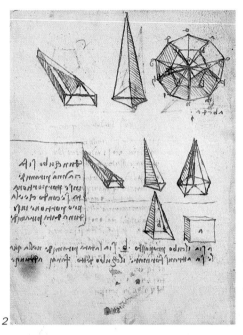

1

2

3

tion of natural phenomena. As such, it had to be studied in depth. The occasion for doing so arose with the arrival in Milan, in 1496, of Luca Pacioli, teacher of mathematics, disciple of Piero della Francesca, and author of a voluminous *Summa di aritmetica* published in Venice in 1494 and immediately purchased by Leonardo, who also noted the price paid, 119 "soldi" (for a book worth about a hundred million lire today).

With the aid of Pacioli, Leonardo advanced, with some difficulty perhaps, through the complexity of Euclid's theorems. Here he had to go beyond those first three books of elementary concepts on which the teaching of geometry was based. With an almost Evangelical sense of humility he resolved one problem after another, proceeding step by step, like a diligent scholar. Already nearly forty-five, he had just finished the *Last Supper*, the work in which he seems to demonstrate an awareness of the need to consider space in geometric, harmonious scanning. After this he was ready to surpass himself in the virtuosity of the geometric and plant motifs for the decoration of the Sala delle Asse in 1498.

Luca Pacioli was finishing the work that was to make him famous, *De divina proportione* (completed in Milan in 1498 and published in Venice in 1509), to which Leonardo contributed with the illustrations: geometric bodies represented in perspective, from the simplest, purest shape (the sphere) to the most complex polyhedron. The models of the bodies were made of glass to show their structure at a glance; an example can be seen in a well-known portrait of Luca Pacioli painted by Iacopo de' Barbari in 1494. For each body Leonardo provides a solid version and a "pierced" one, portrayed in lattice-work to indicate its structure. Subsequently he was to em-

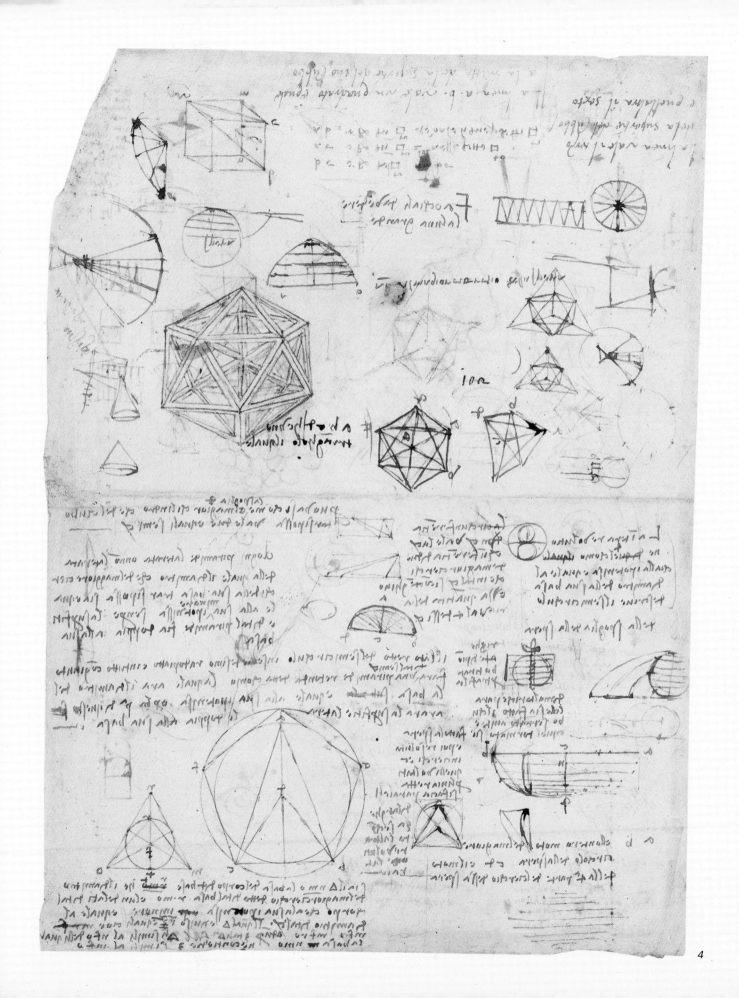

4

1.-2. Geometric
  proportions applied
  to the human
  figure
  Windsor RL 19132 r
  Windsor RL 19136 r
  c. 1490

3. Studies of
  proportions
  of the head
  and human figure
  Windsor RL 12001 r
  c. 1490

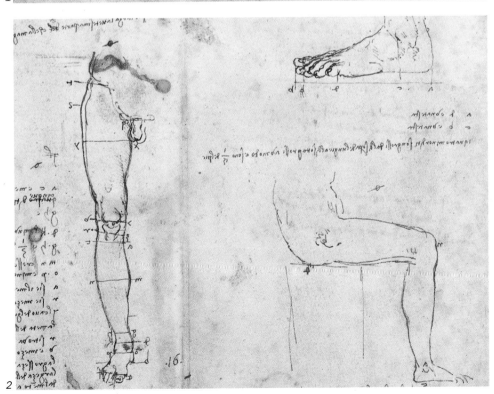

1

2

ploy a similar method in the schematic representation of muscles, reduced to chords indicating the lines of force.

In these illustrations for Luca Pacioli's *De divina proportione* converged all of the intellectual currents of the 15th century, from the experiments of Paolo Uccello to those of Piero della Francesca, from the concepts on proportions expounded in the texts of the Scholastic authors to the Platonic-theological symbology underlying Marsilio Ficino's philosophy. For Leonardo it was not only an exercise in graphic abstraction, but a way of reconsidering the question of the modular principles of architectural shapes, which form the basis for processes of geometric manipulation of space. It is not merely by chance that Bramante was at the same time completing the apse of Santa Maria delle Grazie, in the refectory of which Leonardo had painted the *Last Supper*. And Pacioli speaks expressly of that work as example of the «new architecture». He also relates a highly revealing episode, that of the stone-cutter in Rome who boasted of being able to carve capitals with unsurpassed skill, but was incapable of sculpting one of the simple forms of a geometric polyhedron.

The recent studies of Augusto Marinoni on Leonardo's relations with Pacioli have contributed significantly to our knowledge of Leonardo's scientific work, in all of its intensity and its limitations. The development of Leonardo's mathematical studies, as regards geometry in particular, can now be traced more clearly. And we can more easily understand the determination and serious intent with which, after his return to Florence, Leonardo dedicated himself to the systematic study of geometry, «most impatient with his brush», as reported by a contemporary. It was a program of study followed by Leonardo under the con-

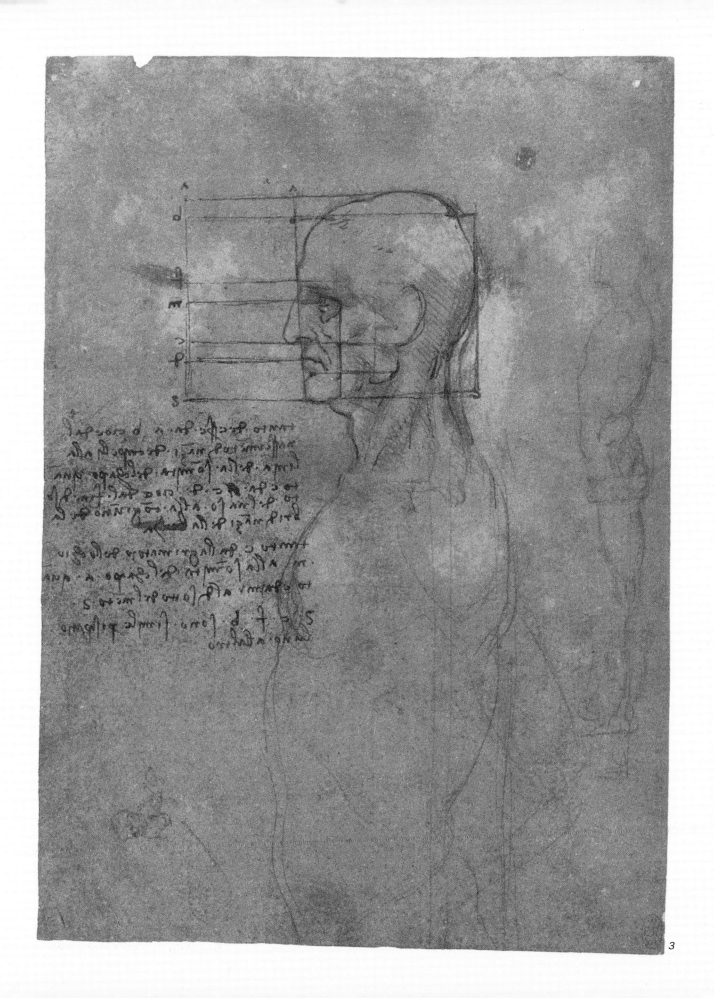

1. Geometric
   proportions applied
   to the study of
   traction: the force of
   the oxen is inversely
   proportional to the
   diameter of the
   wheel to be pulled
   CA f. 561 r
   c. 1487-1490

2. Parabolic
   compass
   CA f. 1093 r
   c. 1513-1514

3. Studies
   of «lunulae»
   CA f. 455 r
   c. 1515

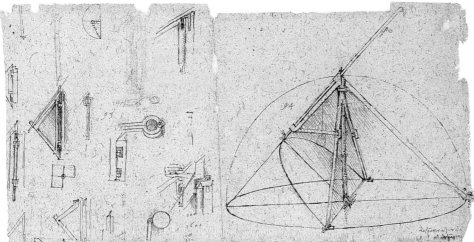

1

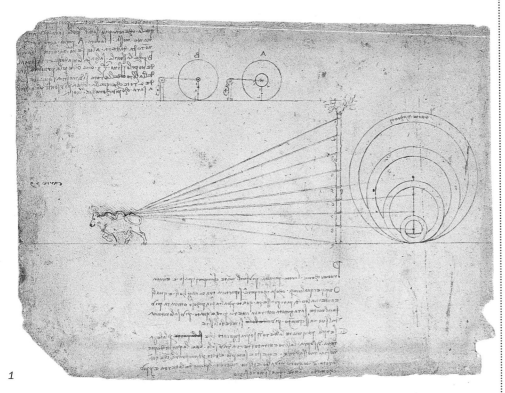

2

stant stimulus of Pacioli, who had returned with him to Florence. Together they worked on a new edition of Euclid which Pacioli was to publish in Venice in 1509, with an acknowledgment to Leonardo for the substantial help he had given in those years.

In the meantime, Leonardo was finding other stimuli in Florence: the scientific encyclopedia by Giorgio Valla published in 1501, utilized by him for to study Hippocrates' «lunulae» and the problem of the «proportional means»; and then the 1503 edition of Archimedes' brief treatise on the squaring of the circle. During this time Leonardo also visited the famous libraries of San Marco and Santo Spirito to consult texts on optics and mathematics, such as those of the Polish Vitellius (Erazm Ciolek) and the Arab Alhazen (Ibn al Haitam). At the time of the *Battle of Anghiari* (1503-1505), traces of exercises on Euclid's theorems can still be found in his manuscripts. But Leonardo was now ready to confront the field of stereometry and the transformation of surfaces, and thus of the «lunulae», a field he was practically never to abandon again until his death in France.

THE THEORY OF FLIGHT

«A bird is an instrument working according to mathematical law, which instrument it is within the capacity of man to reproduce with all its movements, but not with a corresponding degree of strength».

After the lengthy but unsuccessful studies on artificial flight conducted in Milan, Leonardo dedicated himself to studying the flight of birds, starting immediately after his return to Florence in 1500. In 1505 he compiled comprehensive observations on the behavior of birds in relation to the wind, many of which he collected in a small codex that also contains notes on me-

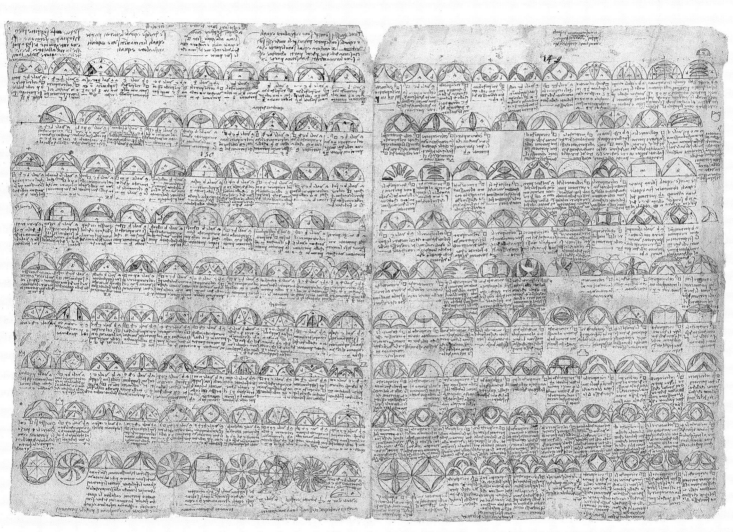

chanics, hydraulics and architecture. The analytical mind of the scientist proceeds by analogy: «That bird will rise up to a height which by means of a circular movement in the shape of a screw makes its reflex movement against the coming of the wind...» Or, in alternating soaring and descent: «They flock together and spiral upward with many turns, and then repeat again their first movement, in a line slanting gently downward; then they flock together again, and rise wheeling through the air».

This is the spiral flight in which Leonardo recognized the vitality of nature. He saw it in whirlpools of water, in the flow of the blood and in wavy hair, as well as in the arrangement of the branches of plants, discovering the law of phyllotaxy which in modern botany bears his name. It was this same vital force that Leonardo expressed, just at that time, in the serpentine lines of *Leda and the Swan*, and in the impetuous whirling of the horses in the *Battle of Anghiari*.

The idea of a glider, a flying machine to be launched in flight from the top of Monte Ceceri, at Fiesole near Florence, also dates from this time, around 1505. In 1550 Gerolamo Cardano was to recall Leonardo's experiments with flight: «He tried to fly but in vain. He was an excellent painter».

The study of flight continued, resumed at intervals, and increasingly based on scientific criteria and a comparative approach: the anatomy of birds as compared to that of man; the motion of the wind as compared to that of water.

From 1510 on, Leonardo conducted further research. «I will show the anatomy of the bird's wings, along with the chest muscles that drive these wings. And I will do the same of man, to show how he can be supported in the air by the beating of wings».

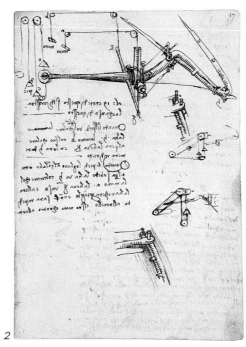

1

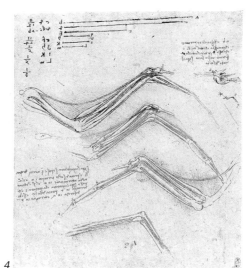

2

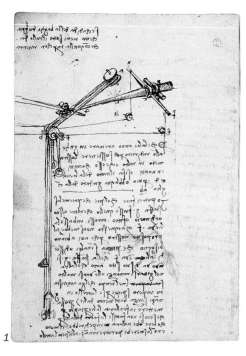

3

4

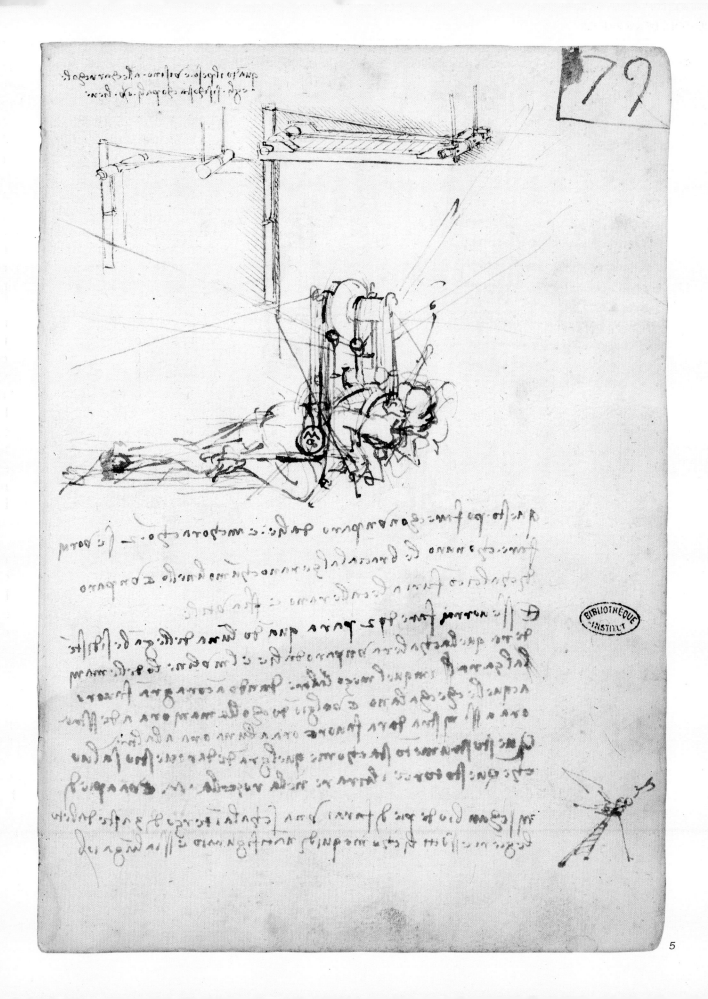

These studies, now at Windsor, are datable to 1513. At that time, surprisingly, Leonardo had returned to the conviction that an aircraft could be lifted by man's muscular strength alone. Only recently a pilot in Pasadena, California, Allen Bryan, has proved that Leonardo was right. In the same late period, around 1513-1514, Leonardo continued to study air currents, and expounded the concept of «true science», i.e., of theory formulated on the basis of observation and experience, according to which the motion of air could be likened to that of water. This is expressed in the famous text cited at the beginning (p. 10), which is a first formulation of the science of fluids.

To the study of water, «Nature's carrier», Leonardo had dedicated himself intensely since the early years of his stay in Lombardy. Already at that time he had touched on almost all of its aspects, but still without the impetus that would make him dream of compiling a treatise on water, in fifteen books, on which he was still working as an old man.

From 1508 on, his studies of water currents and whirlpools were marked by increasingly exuberant vitality. But the strict accuracy of their geometric schemes is unable to restrain them within the bounds of mere illustrations to a text. Soon they overflow in a majestic vision of terrifying floods, leaving no space for a written text. They are transmuted into images of pure energy encompassing all of the elements, a manifestation of destruction that is a part of the natural process of change. Everything is overwhelmed in a well-orchestrated fury: plants, men, animals. The beings of the perceivable world, minutely and lovingly studied in the past, are hurled into the oblivion where nature claims supreme sovereignty.

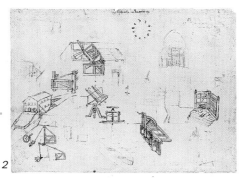

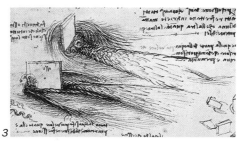

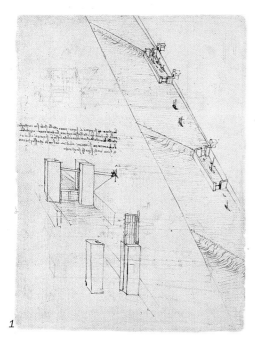

It is known that Leonardo invented various instruments to facilitate the work of artists. These instruments, which were used even by Albrecht Dürer, are in fact mentioned in his will.

The perspectograph, already mentioned by Leon Battista Alberti and represented an early sheet of the Codex Atlanticus is a forerunner of the camera insofar as it provides the artist with an exact reproduction of reality. As such it is often taken as symbol of scientific research, and it has been suggested that the figure of the young observer in the drawing is the artist himself.

THE PERSPECTOGRAPH AND THE ELLIPSOGRAPH

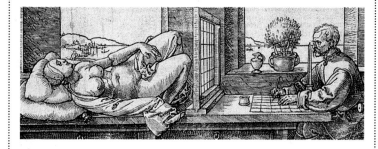

Above, Dürer's perspectograph 1525
Lower left, perspectograph, CA f. 5 r
c. 1480-1482

Below, adjustable-opening compasses
Ms H f. 108 v, c. 1494
At left and below, models of adjustable-opening compasses and of the ellipsograph (Bologna Exhibition of 1953)

consists of three legs forming a triangle and a stylus-carrier rod used to inscribe perfect ellipses. It was designed to be used for precision mechanisms such as the oval-shaped wheels in planetary clocks, some examples of which can be seen on f. 24 r of the Madrid Ms I.

In a codex by Benvenuto di Lorenzo della Golpaja now in Venice – a collection of drawings of inventions by his father and numerous other contemporaries, among them Leonardo – appears, with the name of its inventor, the adjustable-opening compass drawn by Leonardo in about 1494 on f. 108 v of the Paris Ms H.

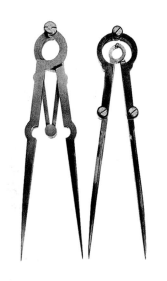

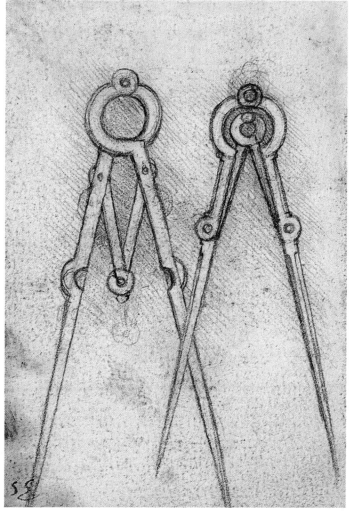

The ellipsograph was known to Arab mathematicians. Leonardo conceived it as a mechanical device capable of presenting the geometric process of conic sections in graphic form. He drew it in several versions, one of which, now lost, was widely diffused and copied a number of times by his contemporaries, among them Dürer.

The instrument, a model of which was created for the Bologna Exhibition of 1953,

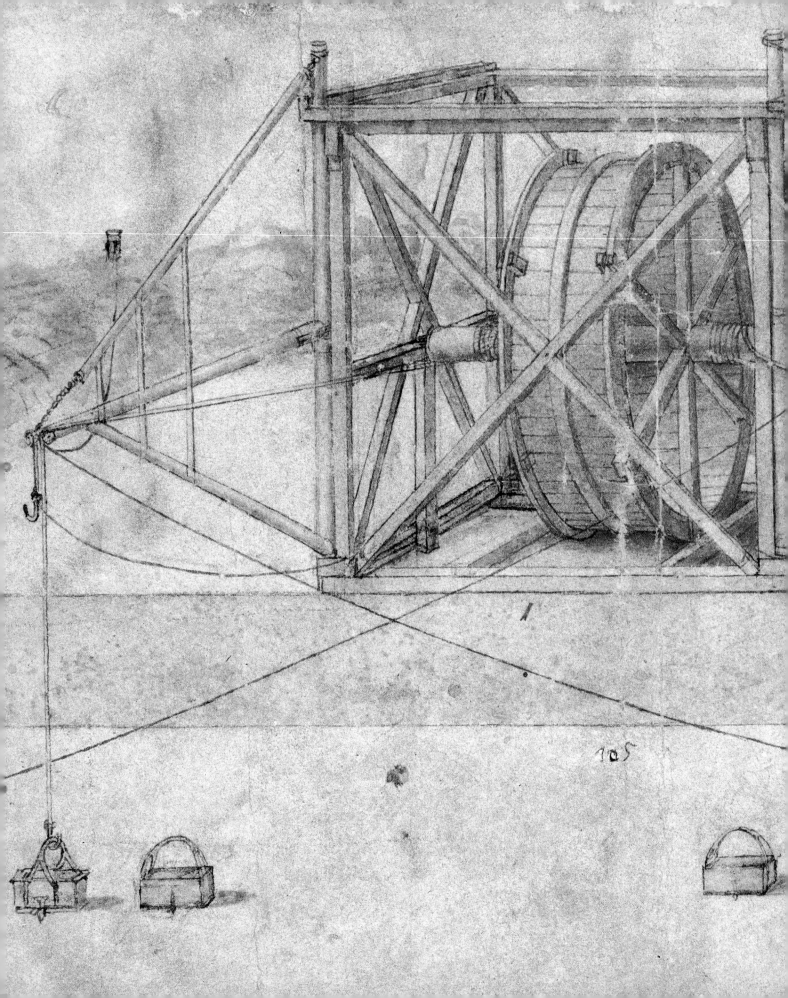

Homo faber

Every one of Leonardo's technological concepts is inspired by the examples of nature. In each of them man, as a living machine, is recognized as the insuperable model of inventive genius which can only in part be simulated by a robot. This is an aspect of Leonardo's technology that has only recently emerged, predominating over the still fascinating subject of his inventions in the military and civil sphere – inventions that range from the armored tank to the helicopter, from the submarine to the automobile all the way to the spectacular excavating machines. Within this context the close relationship seen by Leonardo between anatomy and technology, which led him to apply the same principles of drawing to both, becomes strikingly evident.

Overleaf, on the two
preceding pages:
detail of
excavating
machine
CA f. 3 r
c. 1503

1.-2. Studies on
mechanics
of the human body
Windsor RL 19040 r-v
c. 1508

3. Diagram of wing
mechanism for glider
CA f. 934 r
c. 1506-1508

4. Studies for an
anatomical
model of leg
with muscles
indicated
by copper wires
Windsor RL 12619
c. 1508

5. Studies of muscles
of the mouth
Windsor RL 19055 v
c. 1508

The *Mona Lisa*, the *Last Supper* and the letter to Ludovico Sforza in 1482 can be taken as a summary of Leonardo's fame the world over: the artistic-scientist and inventor. To understand his art we must follow his thought through its systematic, passionate exploration of nature and its laws, as expressed in his manuscripts and drawings. It then becomes clear that art was for him a form of creative knowledge which went beyond science. It was a higher means of expressing human feelings – of «mental motions», – the essence of which was to be found in the smile.

The smile is, in fact, produced by complex imperceptible movements of the facial muscles that no machine can ever replicate. Leonardo was aware of this. It was the motions of the twenty-four muscles of the mouth that he proposed to describe and portray, «testing these motions with my mathematical principles». The same method was applied in his anatomical studies from 1508 to 1510, where he began to consider the relationship between the human machine and the one invented by man.

From this emerges a portrait of himself as inventor: «Although human ingenuity makes various inventions, responding with different instruments to a single objective, never will it find an invention more beautiful, more facile, nor more direct than those of nature, because in her inventions nothing is lacking and nothing is superfluous».

THE MECHANICAL LION

The invention of Leonardo that made the most striking impression on his contemporaries is the one of which no trace has remained, not even a note in his manuscripts: the mechanical lion. Only recently has it been learned that the automaton was

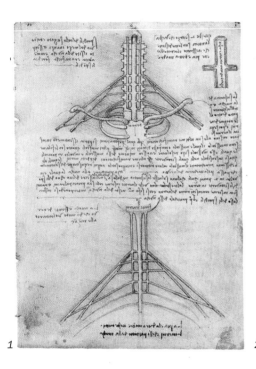

1

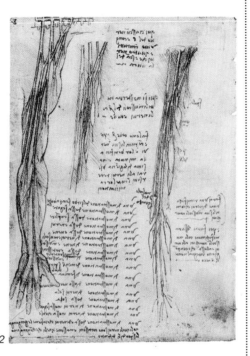

2

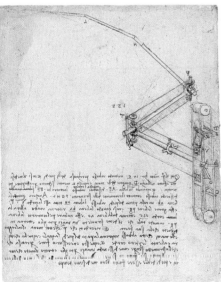

3

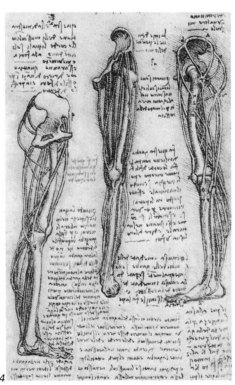

4

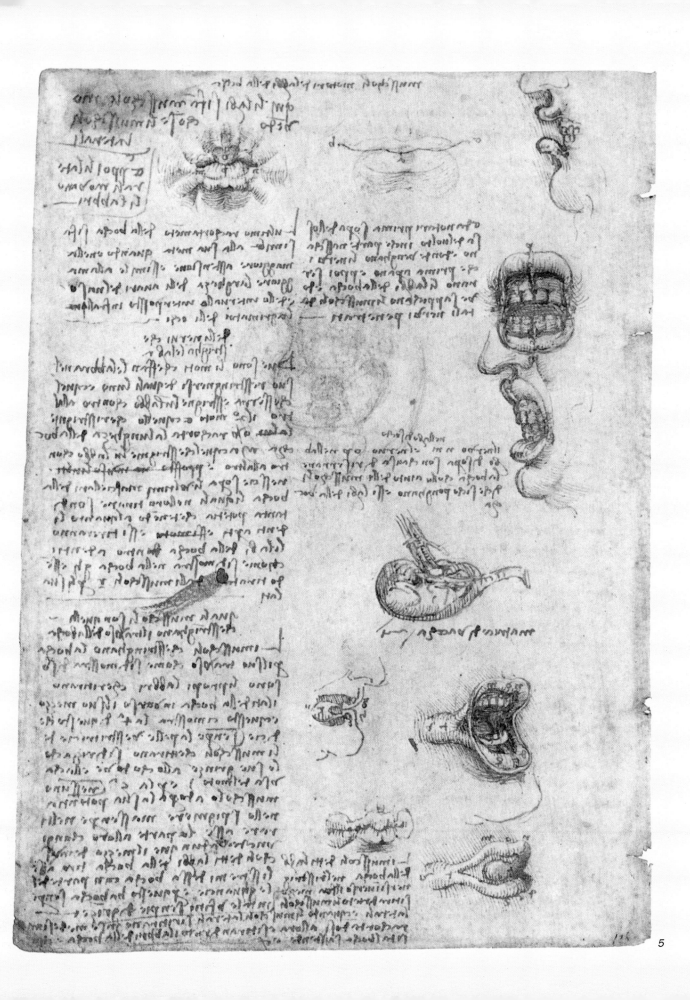

1.-2. Studies
   of lion's heads
   Windsor RL 12586,
   RL 12587
   c. 1500-1503

3. Study of parade
   helmet
   in the jaws
   of a lion
   Windsor RL 12329
   c. 1517-1518

4. Study of fantastic
   animal,
   probably idea
   for an automaton
   Windsor RL 12369
   c. 1515-1516

1

2

3

constructed at Florence in 1515 and sent to Lyon to greet Francis I, the new King of France, upon his triumphal entry into that city.

The festivities were organized by the Florentine colony, which explains the choice of a lion as reference to their adoptive homeland. There was however a double meaning. The symbolic homage was addressed to the powerful monarch with whom the Medici Pope, Leo X, was anxious to ally himself. He did in fact manage to arrange a marriage between the king's aunt, Filiberta di Savoia, and his brother Giuliano de' Medici, Leonardo's protector. So Leonardo had to invent another political allegory, this time recurring to technology. The governor of Florence who commissioned this work of him was the Pope's nephew, Lorenzo di Piero de' Medici, for whom Leonardo also designed a splendid palace that was to have been built beside the old Palazzo Medici.

The lion was the symbol of Florence, like Donatello's *Marzocco* (and had a double meaning: lion-Leo X). The idea was to have the automaton walk toward the king, halt in front of him, rise on its rear legs and open its chest with its front paws to show that in place of a heart it bore the lilies of France, the same lilies that Louis XI had granted to the Florentine republic in the 15th century. This symbolic act was to sanction the renewed friendship between the two nations.

In 1584 Giovan Paolo Lomazzo spoke of this automaton as an «admirable artifice», noting on another occasion that Leonardo could teach the way «to have lions walk by way of wheels». It is probable that the structural details of the mechanism were described and illustrated by Leonardo in manuscripts now lost. A replica

4

1. Benvenuto di Lorenzo della Golpaja, water meter designed by Leonardo for Bernardo Rucellai Codex Marciano 5363 f. 7 v c. 1510

2. Sketch of Rucellai machine CA f. 229 r c. 1510

3. Scale working drawing of Rucellai machine according to the measurements specified by Golpaja (from C. Pedretti in "Raccolta Vinciana" Sect. XVII, 1954, pp. 212-213)

4. C. Pedretti: draft model for the Rucellai machine (1953)

5. Studies for Bernardo Rucellai's water meter Ms G f. 93 v c. 1510-1511

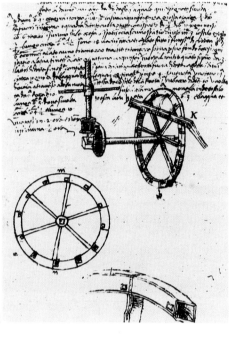

1

2

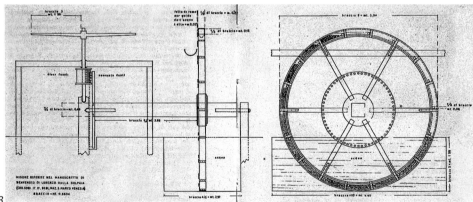

3

4

of that lion was in fact used in the festivities for the wedding of Maria de' Medici and Henri IV, King of France, in 1600. In the published report of that event Leonardo's previous invention is mentioned with an explanation of the circumstances. This is still further proof of the diffusion of Leonardo's technological ideas after his death, a point which should be emphasized.

CONCRETE ACHIEVEMENTS

Fifty years have now passed since I discovered the only document proving that a machine invented by Leonardo had been constructed by him. This was a water meter which he had built by a Domodossola artisan in about 1510 and sent to the merchant and humanist Bernardo Rucellai in Florence, probably to be used on his Quaracchi estate. The instrument is described by one of Leonardo's contemporaries, on the basis of the working drawings it seems, since the measurements are given for each component.

The document which I published in 1952 is a codex by one of Leonardo's contemporaries, Benvenuto di Lorenzo della Golpaja, now in the San Marco National Library at Venice. Two other inventions by Leonardo are described and illustrated: the adjustable-opening compass, which appears drawn by Leonardo himself in one of his notebooks from 1493-1494 now in Paris, and an ingenious compass used «to make an oval», i.e., an ellipsograph probably designed for use in manufacturing oval wheels for planetary clocks. The idea was taken up by Albrecht Dürer and was then diffused in Germany, as proven by a drawing of his at Dresden (see insert on p. 49, above).

The museums of Leonardo's machines which have sprung up all over

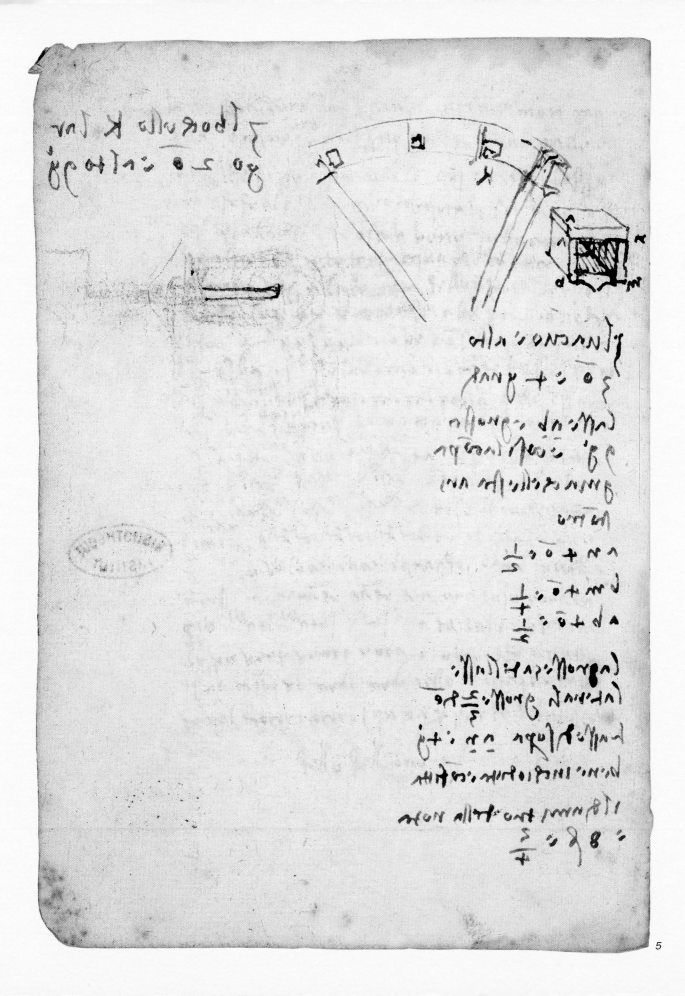

1. Studies of naval
   artillery
   Windsor RL 12632 r
   c. 1487-1490

2. Drawings of military
   machines
   Windsor RL 12647
   c. 1487-1490

the world in recent years – from Italy to France, from America to Japan – insist on presenting models based on drawings by Leonardo which are directly related to the various inventions of military nature listed in the famous letter to Ludovico Sforza.

In addition, there are models of flying machines (mostly of the ornithoptic type, with beating wings, rather than the gliding type), nautical devices such as diving suits and special equipment for underwater connections, machines for excavating channels, hydraulic machines, and so on; in general, all of the most spectacular items that can be taken from his manuscripts, classified by subject rather than chronologically. The extraordinary development of Leonardo's technological activity would instead be shown more clearly in a chronological arrangement.

MACHINES AND DEVICES

The discovery of the Madrid manuscripts in 1967 has contributed still further to incrementing Leonardo's technological repertoire, especially in the sector of textile machines and clocks, as well as devices belonging to the category of «mechanical elements», those which carried out a primary function, such as levers, wheels, gears, etc.

The first of these codexes is the one that contains the most eloquent examples of Leonardo's inventiveness in this sector, the best demonstration of how to present a technological idea through visual language.

These drawings date from about 1497-1500, during the period following that of the *Last Supper* and the studies for the equestrian monument to Duke Sforza. Now famous among them is the full-page drawing illustrating the principle of transmission of motion from a spring for clocks,

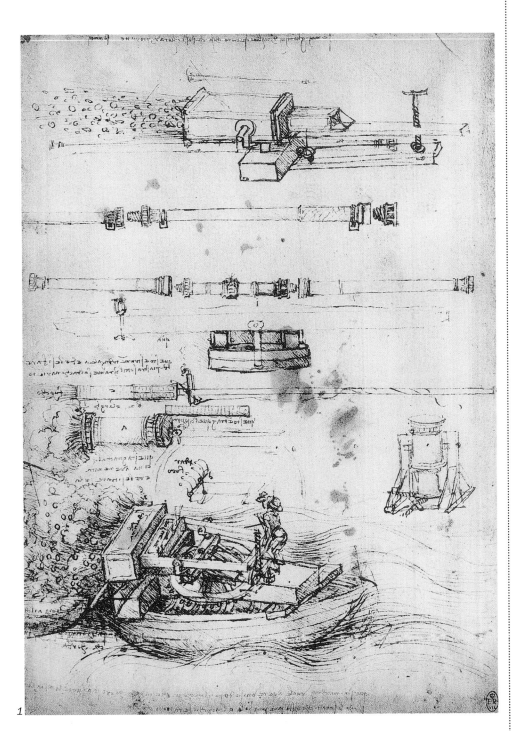

1

1. Reverse screw
   and steering device
   for cart
   Madrid Ms I f. 58 r
   c. 1495

2. Spring-driven motor
   Madrid Ms I
   f. 14 r
   c. 1495

3. Circular worm screw
   Madrid Ms I f. 70 r
   c. 1495

4. Model of
   spring-driven motor
   Florence,
   Museum of History
   of Science
   1987

5.-6. Worm screw
   engaging
   a toothed wheel
   Madrid Ms I f. 17 v
   and functioning
   model
   Florence,
   Museum of History
   of Science
   1987

7. Studies of
   «mechanical
   elements»
   (levers
   and springs)
   Madrid Ms I
   ff. 44 v-45 r
   c. 1497

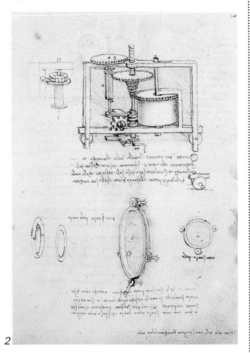

1

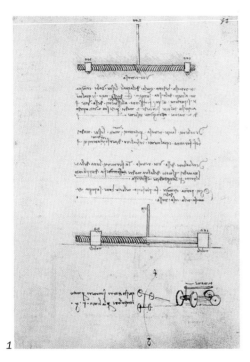

3

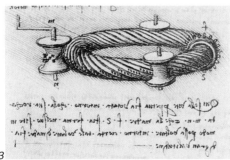

2

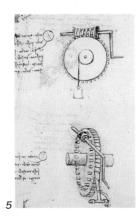

5

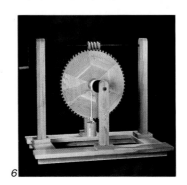

4

6

wound and enclosed in a drum. Here Leonardo demonstrated how motion could be transmitted through a volute spring to compensate for the decreasing force of the spring as it unwinds. The note is limited to information on its construction. The explanation of its functioning is instead entrusted to the drawing, so appropriate in its vigorous, precise lines and at the same time as imposing as that of an architectural monument.

Similar architectural characteristics appear in the drawing of the device shown on the following page. It is hard to imagine what this device could be used for, although its horizontal section and elevation views are clearly drawn. A number of vertical rods are arranged in a circle around a central opening in a circular platform. Each of them is hinged so that it can move outwards along a radius starting from the center of the platform. Problem: how to open the rods simultaneously as if they were the poles of an enormous umbrella-like tent. Solution: a system consisting of a continuous rope passing through a double array of pulleys, the outer ones fixed to the platform, the inner ones mobile but fixed to the base of a pole. As the ends of the rope are wound up on a crank, a uniform pressure is exerted on the inner array of pulleys, controlling the poles as they open out simultaneously.

The brief note accompanying the drawing merely observes that «the wheels toward the center are movable, while those near the greater circle are stable», so that «a circular motion results from turning the crank because the inner rollers draw nearer to the outer rollers and pull anything attached to them».

A glance at the illustration shows that this explanation is superfluous. The drawing is self-explanatory. The

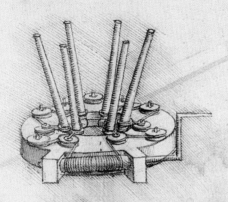

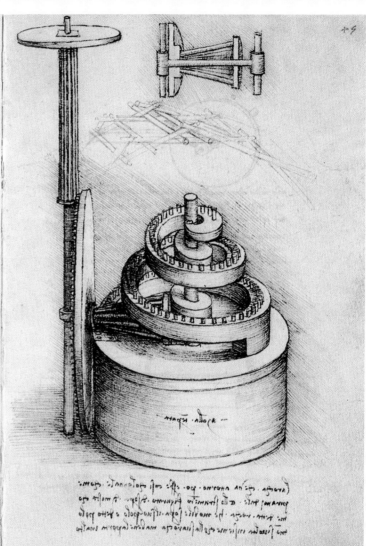

1

2

3

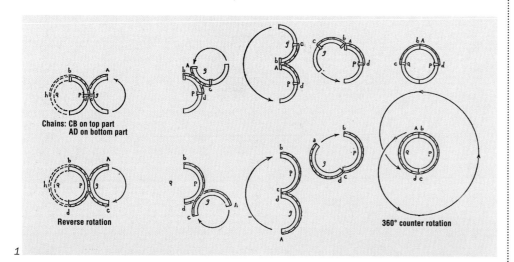

4

same can be said of other examples taken from the same manuscript, like those presented as illustration of the relevant models reconstructed for Leonardo exhibitions and museums all over the world.

CONFRONTATION WITH ANTIQUITY

One little-known aspect of Leonardo's technology is his interpretation of a technological reference in a classical text. In this case the theme of «mechanical element» comes from a literary source, Pliny's *Naturalis Historia*. Pliny's text merely reports that the wealthy Roman building contractor Curius constructed a grandiose wooden mobile theatre made of two rotating halves that could be turned back-to-back, providing two amphitheatres for the simultaneous performance of two plays. The two halves of the theatre could be rotated without disturbing the audience in any way. Pliny reports only this, with no other details. Leonardo took this information and presented it as a problem: «I find among the great Roman works two amphitheatres which were placed back-to-back and then, with all of the audience, were rotated to close together in the form of a theatre».

The following explanation is only a description of the motion of the two amphitheaters diagrammed in horizontal section: back-to-back, aligned and, in the largest format, viewed back-to-back as well as closed to form a circle. In the main drawing Leonardo has traced a perspective view of the entire system in the closed position.

It seems impossible, but Leonardo had succeeded where others, some of the most famous architects and engineers of the 16th century, were to fail; and these were interpreters of

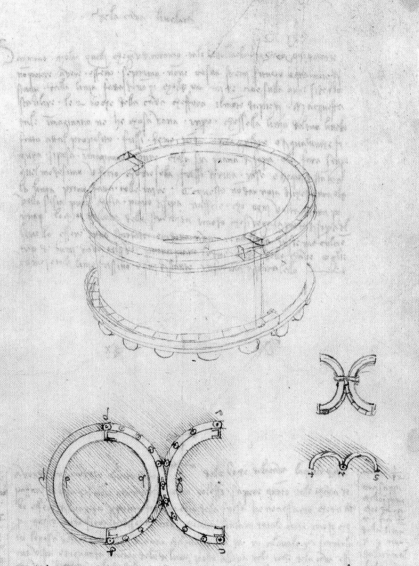

1. Bernardino Luini,
   Child Playing
   with panels held
   together
   according
   to the principle
   of Curius' theater
   as interpreted
   by Leonardo.
   Location unknown

2. Model of ball
   bearing
   Florence, Museum
   of History of
   Science, 1987

3. Ball bearings
   Madrid Ms I
   f. 101 v
   c. 1495-1497

4. Model of ball
   bearing,
   Florence,
   Museum of History
   of Science
   1987

5. Ball bearings
   Madrid Ms I
   f. 20 v
   c. 1495-1497

1

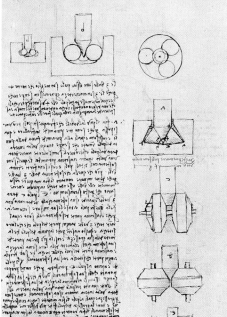

2

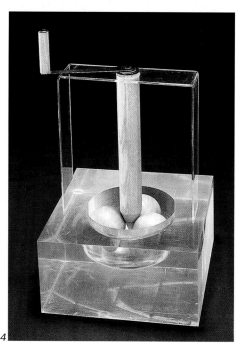

3

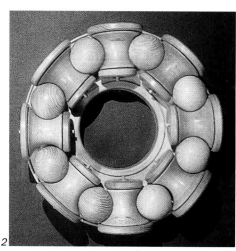

4

Pliny and Vitruvius such as Daniele Barbaro, Francesco Marcolini da Forlì, Andrea Palladio and Gerolamo Cardano. Leonardo demonstrated that imagination and fantasy are as vitally important to the technologist as to the painter. The mechanical principle in fact – the «mechanical element» to be sought for in the classical text – is the same applied in the ancient toy consisting of two panels held together by three ribbons and opening alternatively so that a slender object like a straw or a piece of paper is always held down by one or two ribbons. Although the procedure is difficult to describe it may be recalled that this device was used in the past as a portfolio. Undoubtedly, Leonardo knew of it. In a well-known painting by Bernardino Luini it appears in the hand of a laughing child.

The two amphitheatres were joined in the same way by chains made of wooden blocks, jointed like those of a bicycle and placed one at the base, the other at the top of the amphitheatres, but in alternation. Here an explanation is not only superfluous but may even be confusing.

The American engineer James E. McCabe, accustomed to working with missiles in the Apollo project, managed to understand Leonardo's drawing without reading the caption, and has made a functioning schematic model of it. The reader may find it interesting to resolve the problem himself, on the basis of the visual data offered by Leonardo's drawing, and then check his own solution against McCabe's explanatory diagrams.

Leonardo's schematic demonstration is purposely limited to the problem posed by Pliny's text. Accordingly, no explanation is given of the motive force employed. It can be easily imagined that the great machine

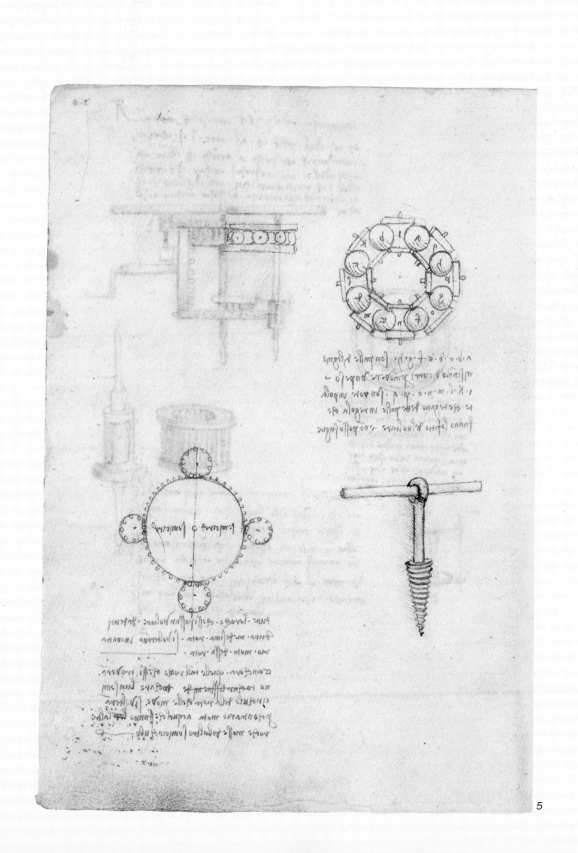

1. Design for canal
   excavating
   machine
   of conventional
   type
   CA f. 3 r
   c. 1503

2. System of
   counterweights
   applied to arms
   of a crane
   Madrid Ms I
   f. 96 r
   c. 1497

3. Studies
   of excavating
   machines
   CA f. 994 r
   c. 1503

was placed on rollers and rotated through cranks drawn by animals. The use of rollers to facilitate motion was known to Roman technology, as demonstrated by the rotating platforms found in sunken ships in Lake Nemi. It is known that Leonardo himself had worked on the problem of friction, and in fact, in the same Madrid manuscript that contains the interpretation of Curius' theater the solution of the modern ball bearing is indicated.

EARTH LOADING AND UNLOADING

Not many machines of large size were conceived and perhaps built by Leonardo, certainly none that could rival the grandiosity of the «great Roman works». Among the few exceptions are the machines for excavating channels, especially those drawn on two sheets appearing at the beginning of the Codex Atlanticus which originally formed a single folio.

A date around the first years of the 16th century is suggested by the style of the large recomposed drawing, so similar, also in the type of heavy paper, to the famous map of Imola of 1502. It is more likely, however, that these two excavating machines relate to the drafts of extensive description or technical reports on the canalization of the Arno River in manuscripts from 1503-1505.

These are drawings which have been damaged by the unfortunate "restoration" of the Codex in the 1960s. Consequently, the notes written by Leonardo as well as the consecutive numbers of the original collector (the ones re-done by the "restorer" are no longer consecutive) have almost entirely disappeared. In my *Leonardo architetto* published in 1978, I reproduced the sheets from old photographs showing them still

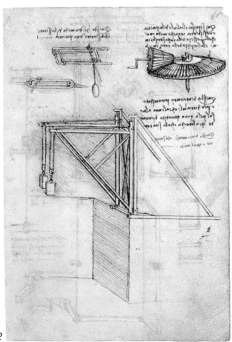

1

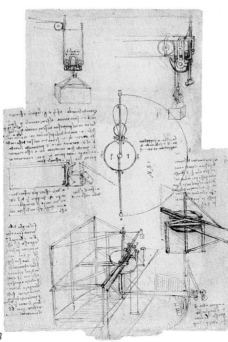

2

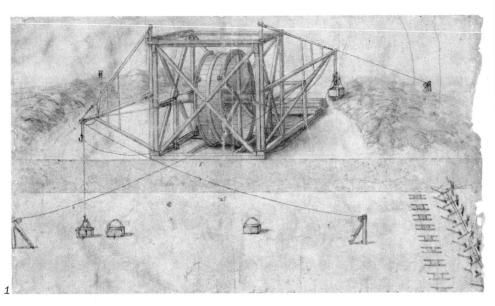

3

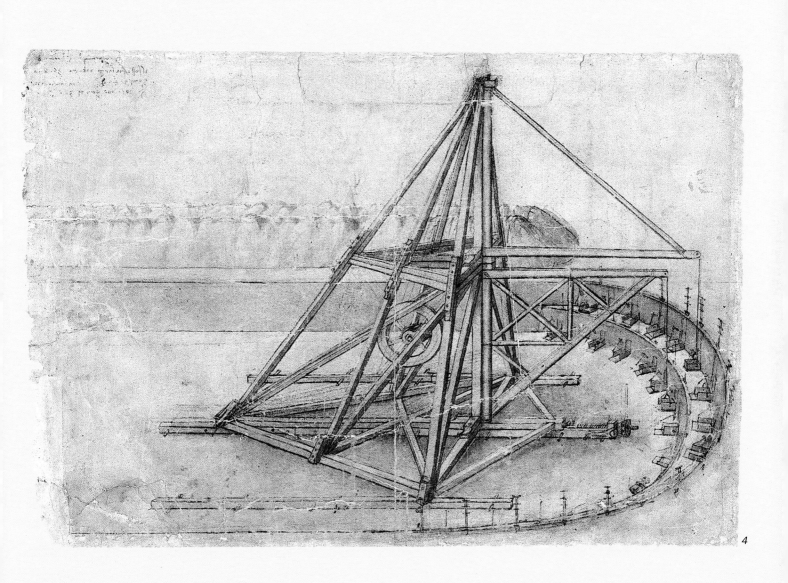

4

1. The «architronito»,
Archimedes'
steam
cannon
Ms B f. 33 r
c. 1487-1490

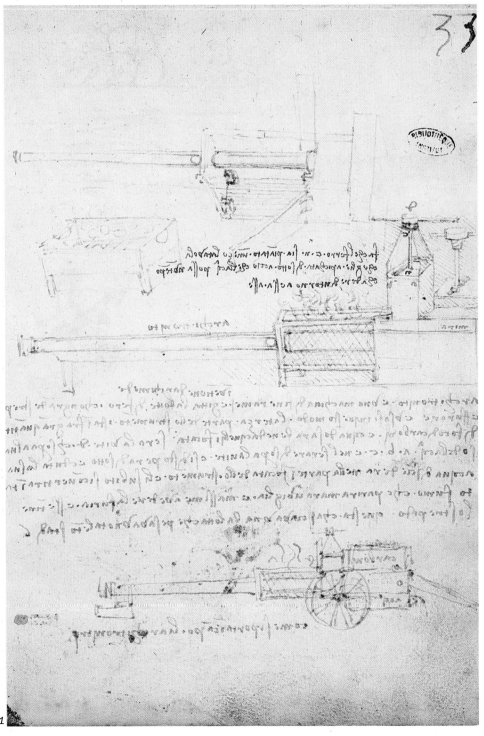

1

intact, allowing them to viewed together as originally drawn by Leonardo. Proof of this is provided not only by the paper and the style but also by the representation of the channel, which is a single drawing running from one sheet to another.

To the left Leonardo depicts the traditional excavator near one of the banks of the channel. It is a system derived from Vitruvius' treatise on architecture, consisting of a drum put in motion by workers who walk inside it to drive the arms of the crane that transports loads of earth piled up by diggers in the ditch.

Obviously, once a certain sector has been excavated the work must come to a halt while the machine is being moved to the next position. Using the technique of "contextual" drawing Leonardo demonstrates the superiority of his own machine in direct confrontation, shown in action on the same canal, to the right. Leonardo's machine advances progressively on tracks inside the canal as the soil is dug by the workers, standing in a semi-circle on two levels of the bank (only their digging tools – hoes and spades – are indicated at the places assigned them). The arms of the crane turn along the same axis to unload the excavated material laterally, onto the banks of the ditch. The small wheel shown at the center of the frame winds up the continuous cable passing from one crane to another. Leonardo devised a highly genial application of the dumbwaiter, as can be verified by notes and drawings found elsewhere in his manuscripts. One box filled with soil rises while the other, emptied, is thrust down by the weight of a worker who jumps into it. The operation is orchestrated to proceed alternatively, and as the excavation goes on, sections of rail are progressively added.

Leonardo had read in Petrarch or some other still unknown source (perhaps the historian and humanist Guglielmo di Pastrengo) that Archimedes built a steam cannon, the «architronito». Leonardo's drawing is almost certainly an example of interpretation of a classical or medieval text.

A similar steam cannon was constructed and used during the American Civil War (see Ladislao Reti, *Il mistero dell'«architronito»*, in "Raccolta Vinciana", XIX, 1962, pp. 171-184).

The industrial application of steam dates back to the early 19th century, starting with the river boat designed by the American Robert Fulton, also famous as the inventor of the submarine.

THE STEAM CANNON

Above, Winan's steam cannon
Below, roasting-jack driven by hot air CA f. 21 r, c. 1480
Lower right, Codex Hammer, f. 10 r c. 1508

Below, "moor's head" (steam-driven bellows), CA f. 1112 v
Right, anonymous, steam-driven bellows (model, Florence, Museum of History of Science, 1995)

Moreover, the properties of steam had undoubtedly been known since antiquity, as exemplified by the "heliocell" of Erone Alessandrino, the steam windmill mentioned also by Vitruvius, which was undoubtedly the embryonic form of the reaction turbines of the future.

Leonardo had studied various aspects of thermal energy, to the point of formulating the principles of the steam-driven machine and even of the internal combustion engine.

But the application of steam to practical purposes was already known in his time.

The famous drawing from his youth of a roasting spit driven by a hot-air turbine already appears in 15th century treatises,

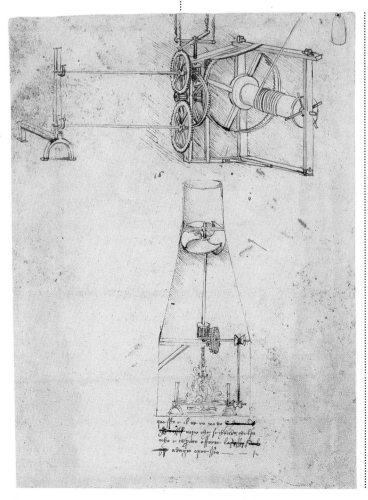

from Mariano Taccola to Giuliano da Sangallo.

Even the device mentioned in the Codex Hammer («The water, which spurts out through the little opening of the vessel in which it is boiling, blows with fury, and is all converted into wind; with this, the roast may be turned») is merely a derivative of Erone's "heliocell", similar to the "moor's head" proposed by Filarete to stir up the fire in a fireplace.

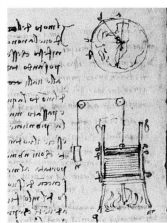

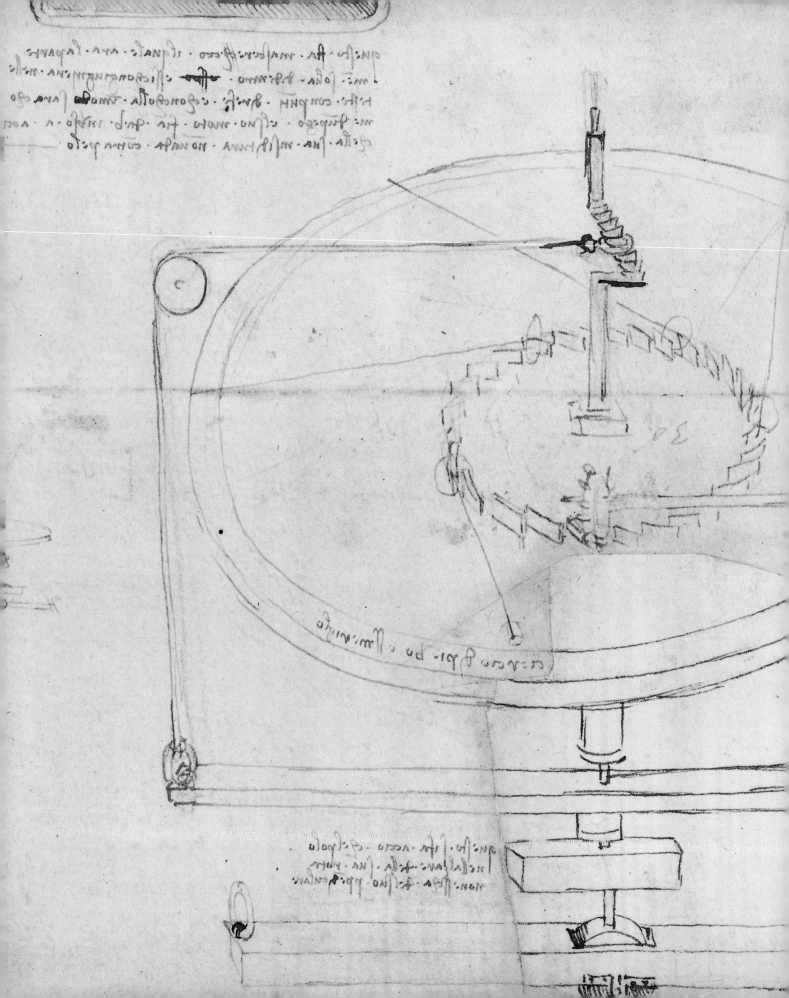

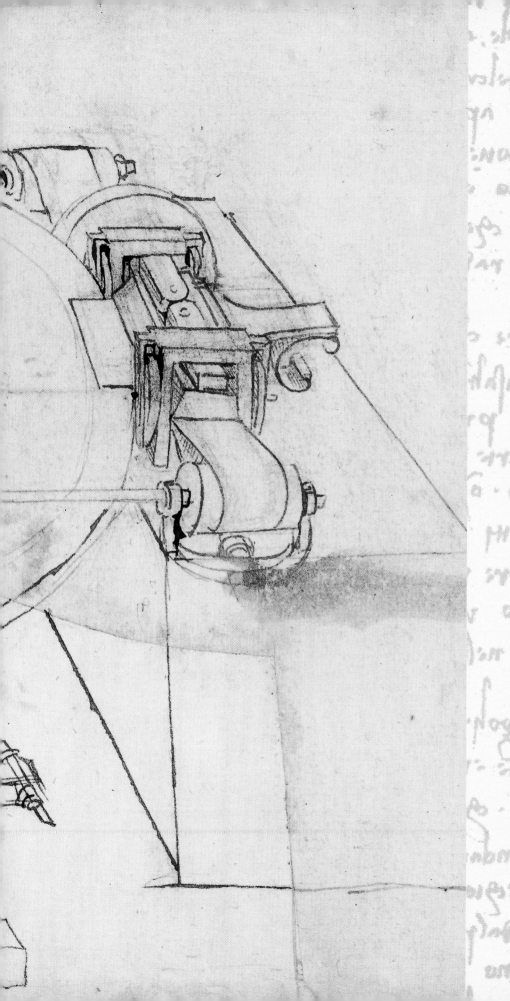

From theatre to industry

Over twenty years of fervent activity in Milan, in the late Fifteenth and early Sixteenth centuries, were marked by prodigious theoretical and practical endeavor in the field of technology. From the painter of the *Last Supper* – and the sculptor of the colossal horse for the Sforza monument – came an inexhaustible outflow of inventive fantasy expressed as organizer of theatrical performances and theoretician of automation applied to various aspects of Milanese industry, the textile sector in particular. From this came numerous proposals for the ingenious perfecting of mechanisms currently in use, as well as futuristic concepts such as flight and underwater navigation, always confronted with an extraordinarily pragmatic attitude.

Overleaf, on the two preceding pages: machine for sharpening needles CA f. 86 r c. 1495

1. Studies for staging of Poliziano's Orpheus

Codex Arundel ff. 231 v-224 r c. 1506-1508

2. Folio of studies for theatrical machine for Poliziano's Orpheus (formerly CA f. 50)

3.-4. Model built in 1964

5. «Ocel della comedia» automaton for theatrical performance CA f. 629 ii v c. 1506-1508

6. Copies of Leonardo's technological drawings, in part lost, first half of the 16th century, Florence, The Uffizi, Gabinetto dei Disegni e delle Stampe, no. 4085 A, c. 1530

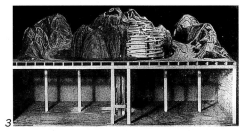

1

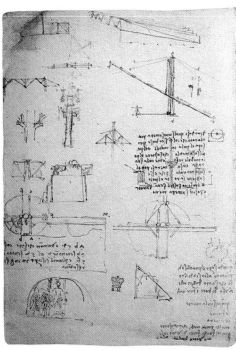

2

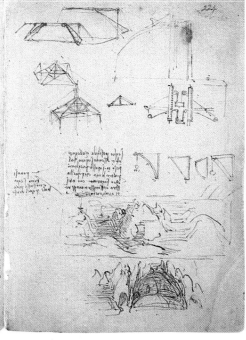

3

4

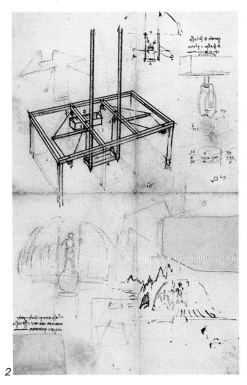

5

The application of the principle of counterweights is suggested in some of Leonardo's other technological drawings (and appears also in the series of «mechanical elements» in the Madrid manuscript). Leonardo himself alludes to it in the famous text previously quoted (p. 52, above), when he says that the superiority of nature in its operations is shown by the fact that it «does not work by counterweights» but has infused a «soul» into the limbs designed to move. The same principle of counterweights was applied by Leonardo to create the rotating stage for the performance of Angelo Poliziano's *Orpheus* in Milan in around 1506-1508. This was a "coup de théâtre" in which a mountain was shown opening while Pluto emerged from the Underworld through an opening in its center. A functioning model of this stage was created in 1964 by the laboratory of the Theatre Department of the University of California at Los Angeles for a symposium on Renaissance theatre organized in that year by the Paris Sorbonne. This model does not yet appear in any of the world's numerous Leonardo museums.

Due importance has instead been acknowledged to a large folio by an anonymous 16th century artist now in the Uffizi drawings collection at Florence, and published by myself for the first time in 1975. It contains nothing less than copies of Leonardo's technological drawings, for the most part lost. Of special importance are the copies of the Munich fragments which had never before been published until I did so in 1957. In these copies the drawings are reproduced before having undergone mutilation.

The stupendous Florence folio, which has shows of the characteristics of a Leonardo original, is important above all as further proof of the dif-

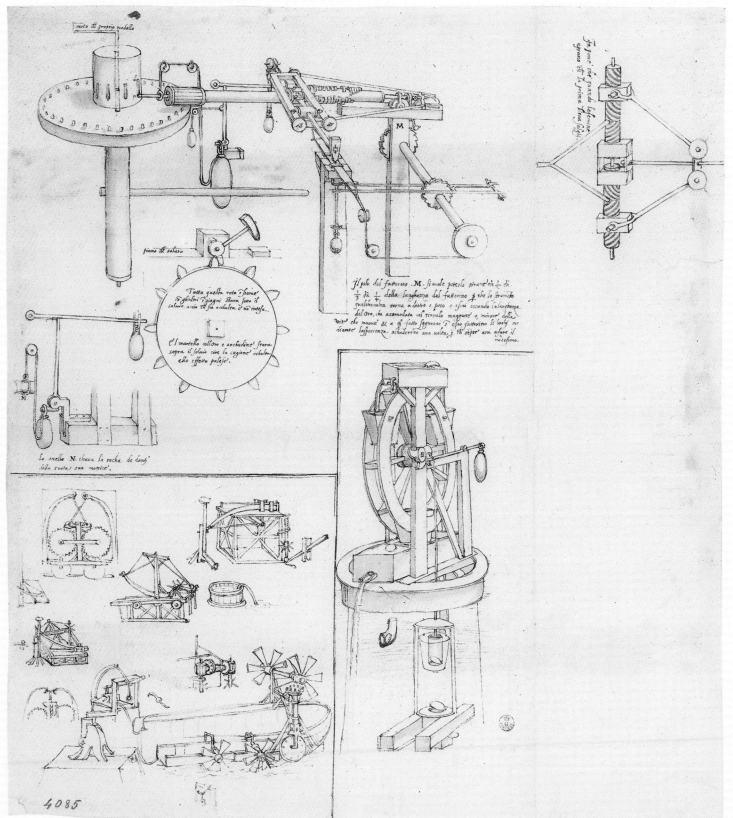

moto di proprio modello

piano di solaro

Tutta questa rota insieme
d'ghisdri d'giegni stara sotto il
solaro, acciò nō sia occulta e nō intesa.

El martello coll'oro e anchadena' stara
sopra il solaro cioè la cagione occulta
ello effetto palese.

lo anello N. chiava la rocta, de denti
della ruota sua motrice.

il polo del fattorino M. si vuole poterlo tirare' er ¼ da
⅓ da ¼ della lunghezza del fattorino e che lo brancio
qualchevolta torna adietro e poco e ssu accendo lalunghezza
del oro, che acomodata coi tircolo maggiore' o, minore' della
vite' che muove' & a gi fatto legname' e osse fattorino il lauij ne
chiame' lasperienza achaderano una volta e tti septe' ara afare il
medesimo.

In questi' vite' quando legitima
apena esi la prima sena sega.

4085

6

1. *Studies of punches for the production of «bisantini» (sequins for evening dresses) CA f. 1091 r c. 1495*

2. *Studies of textile machines for spinning with tab spindle CA f. 1090 v c. 1495-1497*

3. *Textile machine for winding reels Madrid Ms I f. 65 v c. 1495*

4. *Large mechanical shearing machine CA f. 1105 r c. 1495*

5. *Machine for twining cord CA f. 13 r c. 1513-1515*

6. *Studies for «battiloro» machine CA f. 29 r c. 1493-1495*

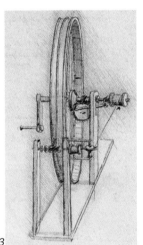

1

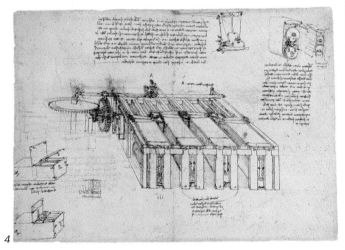

2

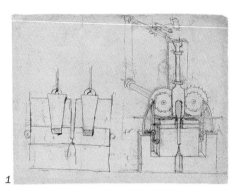

3

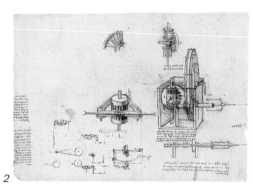

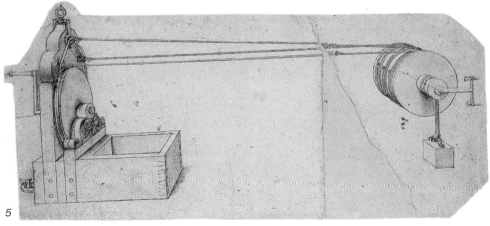

4

5

fusion of Leonardo's technological concepts after his death. The drawing at the top, which reproduces the largest Munich fragment prior to its mutilation, refers to a series of studies made by Leonardo for a «goldblater», a machine for the industrial production of «bisantini», or metal sequins to decorate ladies' evening dresses. The series is datable to about 1495 and suggests Leonardo's participation in the development of the textile industry in Lombardy. The extensive studies on textile machines, automatic reeling devices, teaseling machines, etc., in the sheets of the Codex Atlanticus, fall within the same chronological period. These machines are frequently seen transposed into models, entirely removed from that historical, economic and social context within which they could usefully viewed, at least for educational purposes.

TECHNOLOGICAL DRAWINGS

In the Florence copy (insert at lower left) are some drawings whose source has been lost but which reveal, by reflection, the youthful character of Leonardo's technological drawings. They trace back, in fact, to a drawing dated 1478 with studies of shepherds for a *Nativity* (see on p. 77) and sketches of mechanical devices on both sides of the sheet. These in turn lead back to other youthful folios in the Codex Atlanticus and elsewhere, including the study of a self-propelled cart still today termed – for the presence of the differential if nothing else – Leonardo's "automobile". (see insert on p. 81, below).

Lastly, the Florence sheet includes a strange kind of boat propelled by wind vanes, which suggested to me a possible reference to Brunelleschi's "Badalone", the legendary river boat invented and even patented by the famous Florentine architect that was to be

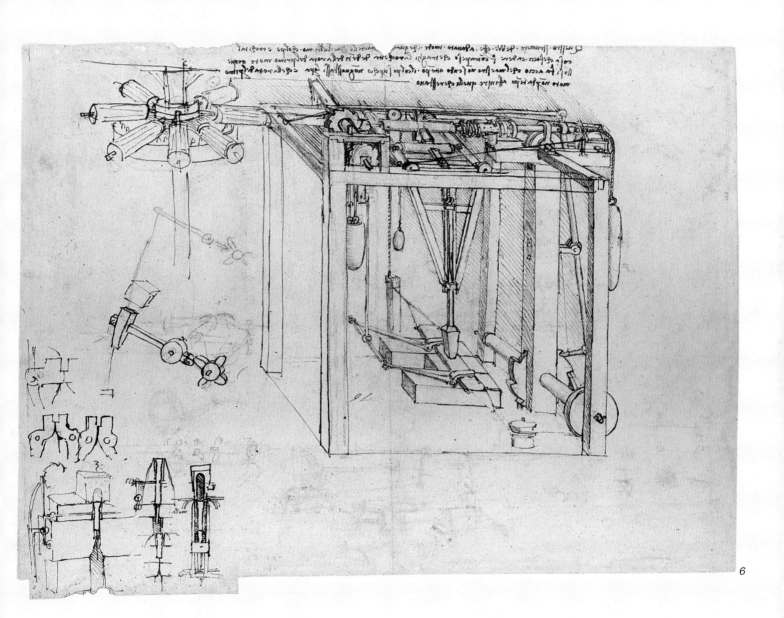

1. Boat driven by wind vanes, copy of lost drawing by Leonardo which probably reproduces Brunelleschi's legendary "Badalone" Florence,

The Uffizi, Gabinetto dei Disegni e delle Stampe no. 4085 c. 1530

2. System for transmitting motion to the axle of a cart

(principle of the differential) CA f. 17 v c. 1478-1480

3. Studies of shepherds for a Nativity and of mechanism for a self-propelled cart

Florence, The Uffizi, Gabinetto dei Disegni e delle Stampe no. 446 E dated «December 1478»

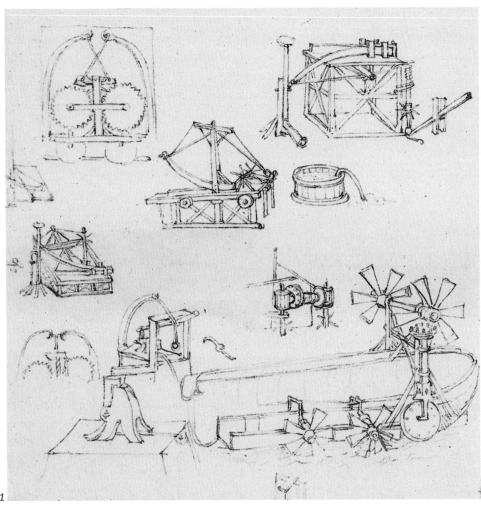

1

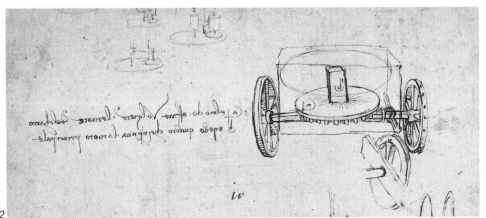

2

used for transporting marble from Pisa to Florence to build the Cathedral dome. It was a failure. The chronicles of the time report that the strange boat ran aground in the basin formed by the Arno River at Empoli, and was abandoned there. Perhaps it still existed in the time of Leonardo, and as a boy he may have gone to see it from the nearby town of Vinci. Although this is only a hypothesis, it may be used to seek in Leonardo's youth for the roots of his great fascination with technology. Soon afterward, as has been seen (p. 16), he was to find in Verrocchio's workshop another contact with Brunelleschian tradition in the construction of the copper ball to crown the cathedral dome.

CONTEMPORARY TECHNOLOGY

Every aspect of Leonardo's technology, from the first to the last machine designs, can be related in some way to the technology of his time. A study of the context to which a design belongs in no way diminishes its importance. On the contrary, it reveals its originality, by revealing the techniques devised by Leonardo to improve existing devices. There is only one field into which he ventured alone: the study and perhaps the testing of flying machines. It is true that the problem of flight had been mentioned already in the 13th century by the learned Roger Bacon (whose works Leonardo knew), while the Paduan architect Giovanni Fontana seems to have studied it in about 1430. And it is also true that attempts at flight seem to have been made toward the end of the 15th century at Perugia, but the news was reported only in the 17th century. No document has yet confirmed that the architect Giovan Battista Danti of Perugia tested a flying machine of his own invention over Lake Trasimeno. Moreover, Leonardo himself suggested that

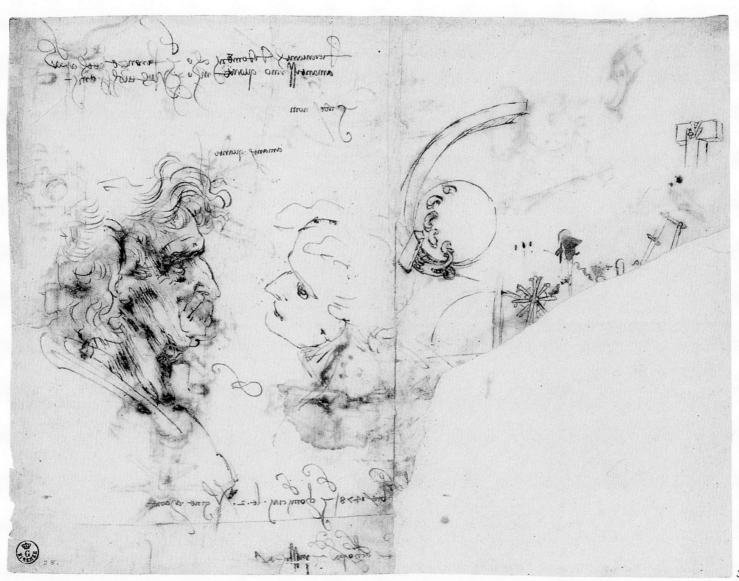

1. Study of
   artificial
   wing
   Ms B f. 74 r
   c. 1487-1490

2. Design of
   ornithopter
   with pilot
   in prone position
   Ms B f. 75 r
   c. 1487-1490

3. Vertical ornithopter
   Ms B f. 80 r
   c. 1487-1490

4. Studies of flying
   machines
   Florence, The Uffizi,
   Gabinetto dei
   Disegni e delle
   Stampe, no. 447 E r
   c. 1480

5. Study of flying
   machine

CA f. 860 r
c. 1480

6. Folio of studies
   on artificial flight;
   upper right,
   sketch
   of parachute
   CA f. 1058 v
   c. 1480

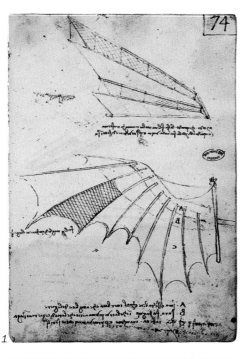

1

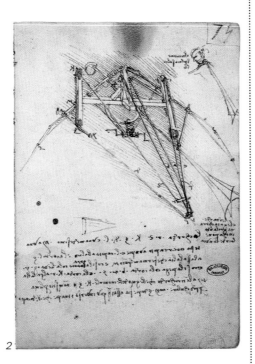

2

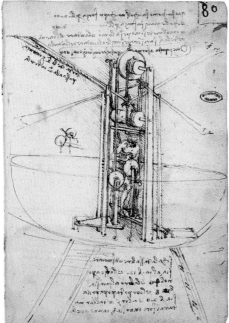

3

4

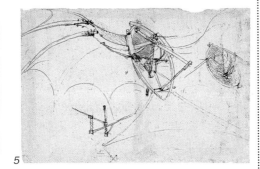

5

his machine should be tested over a lake to avoid the danger of a possible fall. It is interesting to note that flight was already being thought of in relation to military architecture. The parachute designed by Leonardo was indicated by him as suitable for leaping down from a great height, such as a tower or the bastions of a fortress. Moreover, Leonardo's known studies on flight, including the helicopter, are found in a Paris manuscript of 1487-1490, the so-called Codex B, largely dedicated to fortifications and weapons. It is also certain that at the time of Leonardo kites were used for reconnaissance purposes, based on models that may have been imported from China, allowing a man to be lifted to a considerable height. Leonardo himself has left us a graphic memorial of this in the first of the Madrid manuscripts (see insert on p. 29, above).

BETWEEN SKY AND SEA

Leonardo began his studies on flight much earlier than has been commonly believed, as early as the time of the *Adoration of the Magi*, in 1481, and thus before going to Milan. This is demonstrated by a drawing in Florence, at the Uffizi, where beside a study of drapery for one of the figures in the *Adoration* appear sketches of mechanisms and a diagram of the gliding flight of birds, as explained in a note: «This is the way birds descend». It is therefore unsurprising that the back of the sheet is entirely dedicated to studies for a flying machine in which the characteristic shape of artificial wings inspired by those of the bat already appears. Although I published these drawings already forty years ago, it is only now that they have received due attention in the contributions of Domenico Laurenza to the chronology of Leonardo's studies on flight. And the submarine? Leonardo must be reco-

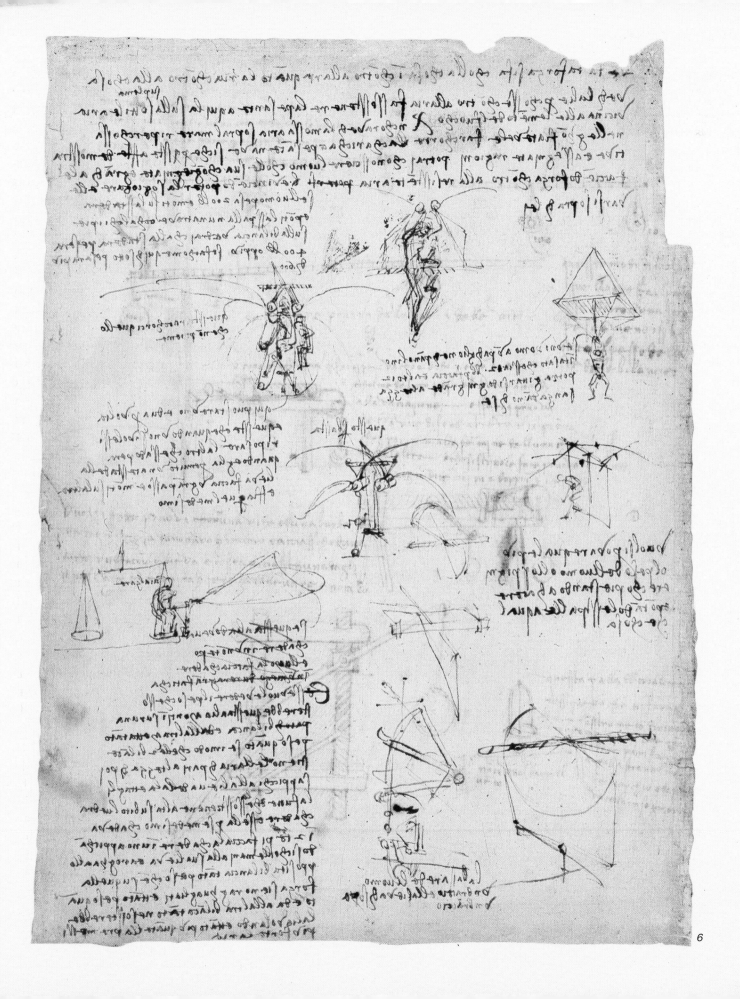

1. Studies for
submarine
CA f. 881 r
c. 1485-1487

2. «Boat
to be used
to sink ships»
Ms B f. 11 r
c. 1487-1490

3. «Breathing
apparatus
for diver»
Codex Arundel
f. 24 v
1508

gnized as the father of this invention, as he himself claimed: «How many stay with an instrument for a long time under water. How and why I do not describe my method of staying underwater as long as I can stay without eating, and this I do not publish and divulge due to the evil nature of men, who would use it to murder at the bottom of the sea, breaking ships at the bottom and sinking them along with the men who are on them. And although I teach other methods, they are not dangerous because the mouth of the reed used for breathing, coming from the wineskins or cork, can be seen above the water». This now famous declaration, in a manuscript datable to about 1506-1508, is often cited as proof of Leonardo's moral stature. It may be considered that Leonardo really invented (and then tested) a submarine, but only to realize the treacherous use to which it could be put. From his studies on the compressibility of air seems to have sprung the idea of a pressurizing system that would allow prolonged immersion. In a folio dating from the first years in Milan he sketches a sort of submergible boat, just large enough to hold a man lying down, who seems to drive the craft through a system of pedals. Another manuscript from the same period contains a sketch of a similar boat, and the accompanying note seems to hint at a method of pressurizing. On the other hand, it might allude to a mention by Cesare Cesariano, a contemporary of Leonardo's, of a craft used to navigate under water from the moats of the Castello Sforzesco in Milan to the Castello di Musso on Lake Como. Cesariano, a pupil of Bramante and author of the 1521 edition of Vitruvius, was in Milan around 1508, at the time when Leonardo was engaged in hydraulic studies and when he declared to himself that he would not divulge his invention of the submarine.

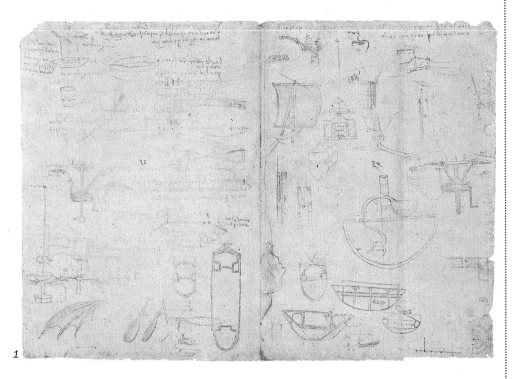

1

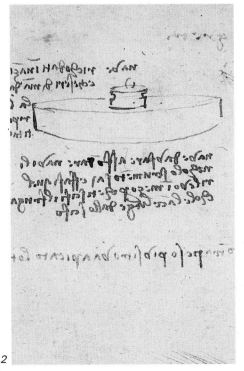

2

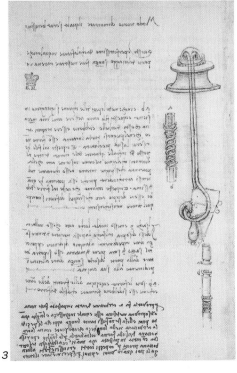

3

The first indication that the sketches on f. 296 v of the Codex Atlanticus are studies for a self-propelled vehicle appeared in an article by Guido Semenza published in 1929. This served as basis for the model built by Giovanni Canestrini for the 1939 Leonardo exhibition in Milan, and for replicas which are still being produced today.

The object in question is a three-wheeled cart with a steering device, in which the great leaf springs have been erroneously interpreted as the source of motive power. The latter is instead furnished by springs wound around the fulcrum of each of the two horizontal wheels, coupled at the center; springs probably placed under those wheels, since they are barely visible in the horizontal section view. Through a complex system the unwinding of the leaf springs could be controlled, keeping efficiency constant and allowing them to be re-loaded alternatively.

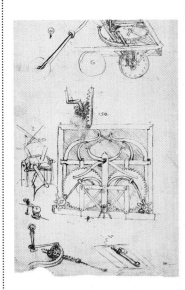

All this has recently been explained by the American Mark Elling Rosheim, a young inventor specialized in robot technology who works for the NASA.

Rosheim has managed to decipher a few brief notes made by Leonardo in 1497, interpreting

THE AUTOMOBILE AND THE LIFE PRESERVER

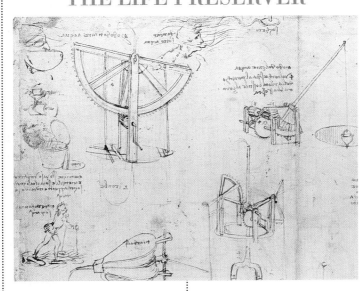

Above, technological studies with system for breathing underwater and a «way of walking on the water», CA f. 26 r, c. 1480-1482
Left, studies of self-propelled cart, CA f. 812 r, c. 1478
Below, study of life-preserver,

them as studies for the construction of a real robot: a mechanical man that walks, moves its arms, sits and opens its mouth to speak. This is reported in "Achademia Leonardi Vinci", IX, 1996, pp. 99-100.

Leonardo's "automobile" was a vehicle designed for short runs, perhaps from one end of a public square to the other. This can be seen in details on the horizontal section view in the Florence copy as well (p. 76, above).

It is probable, as Rosheim suggests, that this is a cart for festivals or the mechanism of an automaton like the mechanical lion

Ms B f. 81 v, c. 1487-1490
Below, study of diving suit, CA f. 909 v, c. 1485-1487
Right, device for air rescue, with wineskins used according to the "air-bag" principle. Codex on the Flight of Birds, f. 16 r, 1505.

created by Leonardo almost forty years earlier.

Leonardo da Vinci's secret method for staying underwater revealed by his manuscripts. Under this title Nando De Toni, in 1939, published the correct interpretation of some enigmatic drawings by Leonardo on two folios in the Codex Arundel dated 1508.

This is not however the submarine Leonardo refers to in the famous text in the Codex Hammer where he states that he will not

divulge his invention «due to the evil nature of men».

It is instead a diver's apparatus. A system of valves for air intake is illustrated and it is specified that the device, equipped with a floater that always reveals its presence, is useful for «calafatare» (to caulk), that is, for performing maintenance and repairing the hulls of ships without having to put them in dry dock.

This is a perfecting, although a highly ingenious one, of devices in use even before Leonardo's time, and already considered by him in his earliest manuscripts, such as Codex B in Paris dated 1487-1490 and in early folios in the Codex Atlanticus.

In the folios of that time Leonardo also showed interest in swimming and maritime rescue, as can be seen in drawings of fins and life-preservers.

There is also a curious system for walking on water.

It is not surprising then that

Leonardo also considered the problem of rescue in case of attempted flight over water. From this came the idea of using inflated wine-skins to protect the body in a fall not only in water but also on land.

One of his notes in the Codex on the Flight of Birds, dating from 1505, is illustrated by a small drawing (f. 16 r) which has only recently been interpreted by Alessandro Vezzosi.

It is the schematic figure of a standing man wrapped in a system of «wine-skins tied together like rosary beads», the principle of the "air bag".

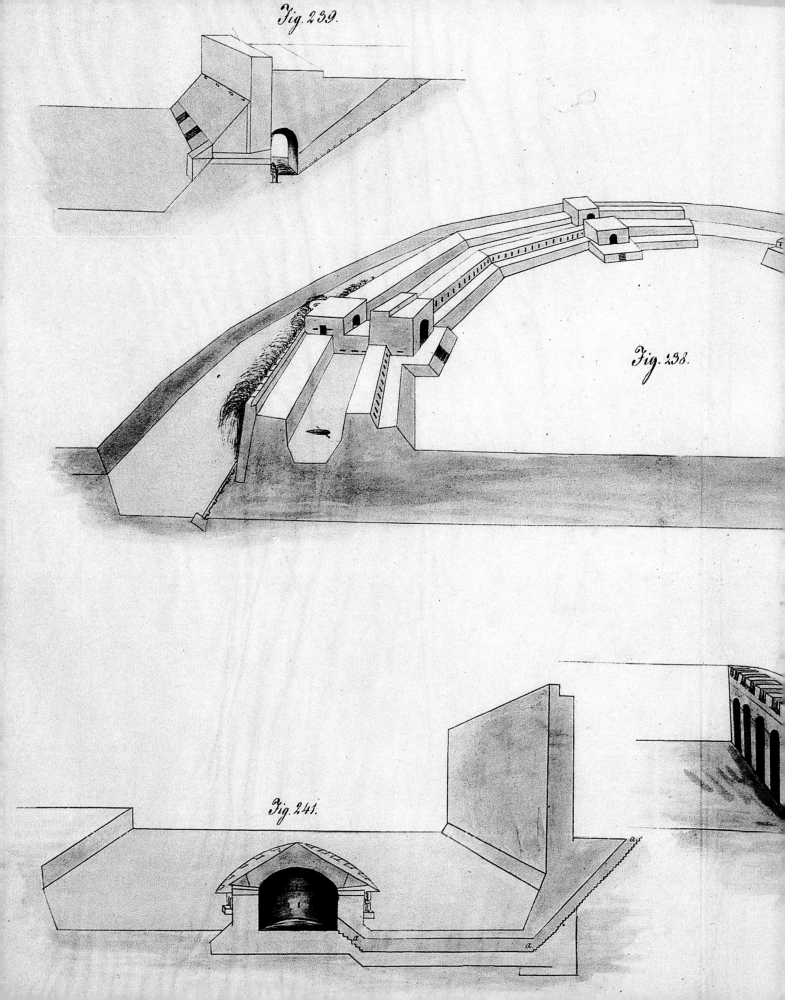

Fig. 239.

Fig. 238.

Fig. 241.

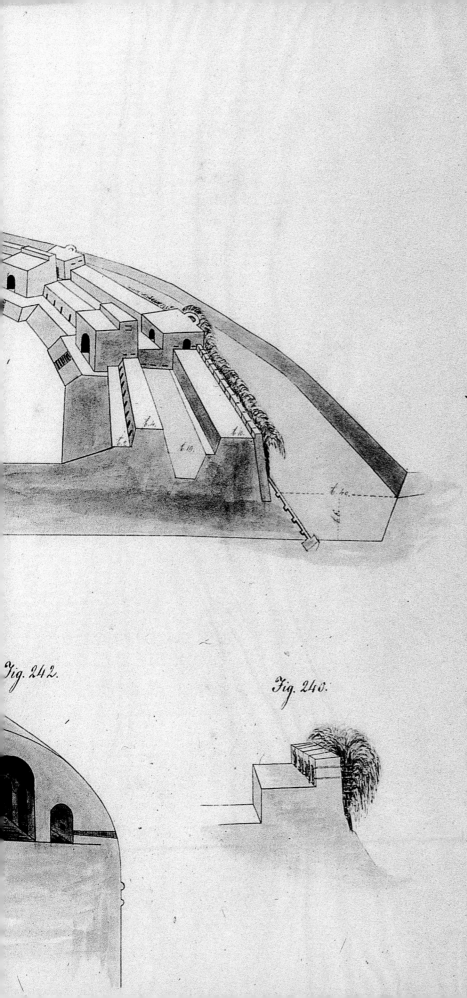

Fig. 242.

Fig. 243.

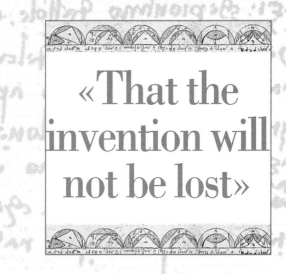

«That the invention will not be lost»

The birth of Leonardo coincided with that of the printing press. Fascinated by typographical presses from the very beginning, around 1480, he studied them already with the innovative idea of an automatic page-feeder, a concept which was to reappear near the end of the Fifteenth Century. With his renewed interest in anatomy in the early years of the Sixteenth Century and with the systematic arrangement of his writings in preparation for compiling numerous treatises, Leonardo become increasingly aware of the need to divulge his inventions through printing. With this in mind he devised a method to be used for the simultaneous reproduction of texts and drawings, three centuries in advance of William Blake.

Overleaf on preceding pages, drawings of military architecture from the Codex Atlanticus copied by G. François and L. Ferrario plate XLI (Milan 1841)

1. Study of typographical press with automatic page-feeder and sketch of kneeling Virgin CA f. 995 r c. 1480-1482

2. Fragmentary sketch of typographical press CA f. 991 v c. 1480-1482

3. Studies for a textile machine CA f. 985 r, c. 1495

4. Details of automatic page-feeder for typographical press on a folio reconstructed from two in the Codex Atlanticus and a Windsor fragment with study of a figure (RL 12722) CA ff. 35 r and 1038 r, c. 1497

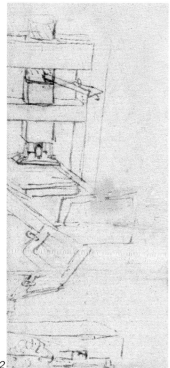

1

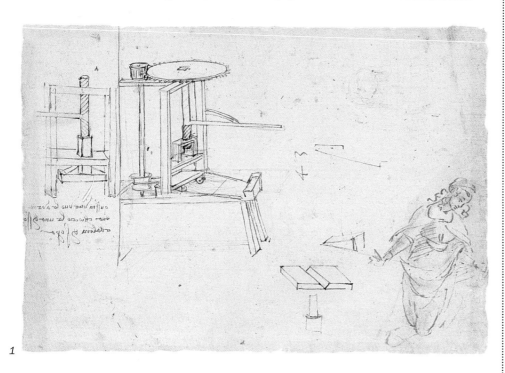

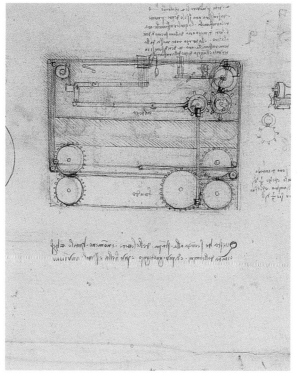

2   3

I will not publicize nor divulge». This statement may be taken, upon reflection, as proof of the fact that Leonardo was accustomed to publicizing and divulging his inventions. Of this we can be certain (and we now have the proof), although the means of communicating information, in his day, were certainly not those of our own mass-media. The printing press made its first appearance in the mid-15th century, just at the time when Leonardo was born. Nothing of his was published while he was still alive.

One of Leonardo's statements in the *Libro di pittura* has been taken as indication of why he did not print his works. It is where he speaks of painting as an art superior to all others, insofar as it cannot be reproduced in copies: «This does not make numberless sons as printed books do».

And yet, in the scientific and technological field, Leonardo had certainly come to recognize the need to find a means of disclosing his ideas and discoveries. A drawing of a typographic press with automatic feeder appears in one of the earliest folios in the Codex Atlanticus, beside the sketch of a kneeling Virgin, probably a study for a *Nativity* or *Annunciation*, datable around 1480-1482. Devices for printing are also mentioned in folios from the last decade of the 15th century.

And there is a real tribute to printing, albeit an indirect one, in a text where Leonardo explains the importance of one of his inventions in the field of textile technology. This appears on a sheet of the Codex Atlanticus datable at around 1495: «This is second to the letterpress machine and no less useful, and as practiced by men it is of more profit and is a more useful and subtle invention».

Later, in about 1505, Leonardo even conceived of a rudimentary system for the simultaneous reproduction of text

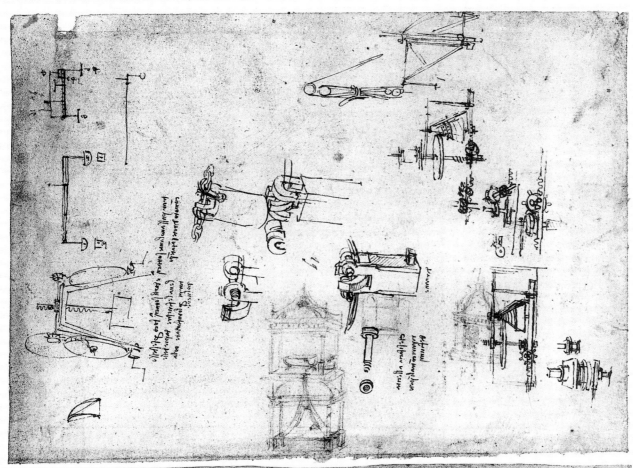

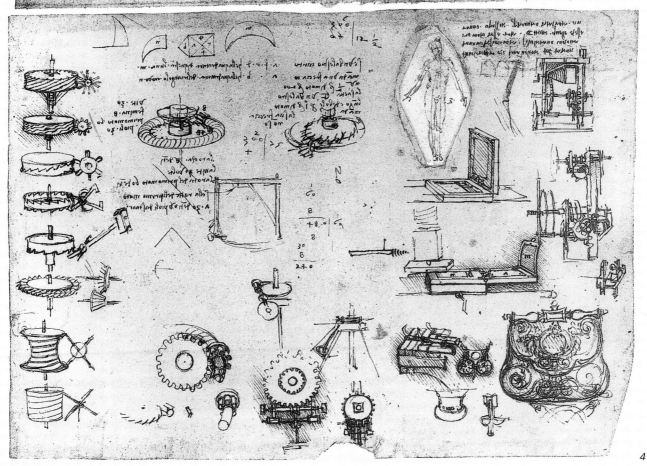

4

1. Clock mechanism:
   example of drawing
   "paginated" for
   printing
   Madrid Ms I
   f. 27 v
   c. 1495-1497

2. Anatomical drawings
   "paginated"
   for printing;
   in the lower
   righthand corner,
   is a note addressed
   to posterity
   Windsor RL 19007 v
   1510

and illustrations, the method that William Blake was to adopt two centuries later (see insert on p. 91, below).

And even later, in about 1515, Leonardo notes his intention of having some of his own works printed, and calculates the number of characters required to compose a book of 160 "carte" (about 320 pages) of 52 lines each, with 50 characters to a page.

PRINTING METHODS

A little earlier, in a sheet from the splendid series of anatomical studies dated 1510 now at Windsor, there is a comment on the need to reproduce those studies through an extremely expensive procedure such as that of engraving on copper. Superb examples of this technique existed but the costs were enormous, as in the documented case of the great and famous «Prevedari print» by Bramante.

Leonardo wrote: «You should make the bones of the neck from three aspects united and from three separated; and so you will afterwards make them from two other aspects, namely seen from below and from above, and in this way you will give the true conception of their shapes, which neither ancient nor modern writers have ever been able to give without an infinitely tedious and confused prolixity of writing and of time. But by this very rapid method of representing from different aspects a complete and accurate conception will result, and as regards this benefit which I give to posterity I teach the method of reprinting it in order, and I beseech you who come after me, not to let avarice constrain you to make the prints in [...]».

The last word is missing because the margin of the paper has been damaged, but it can only be «wood», referring to the xylographic procedure, which is effective as graphic illustration but unable to render the complex

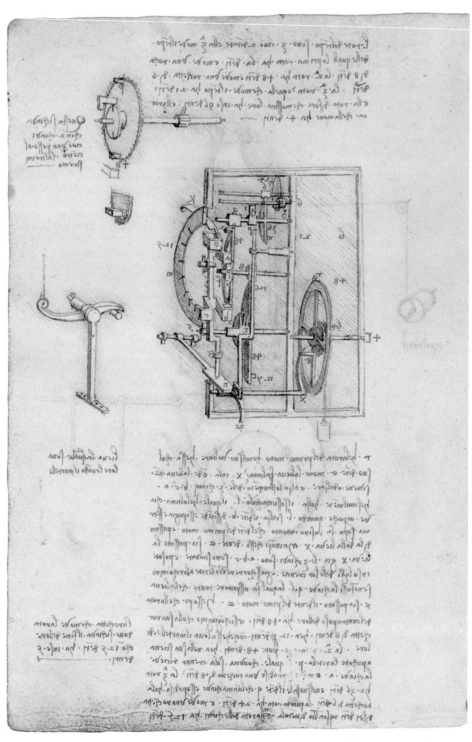

1

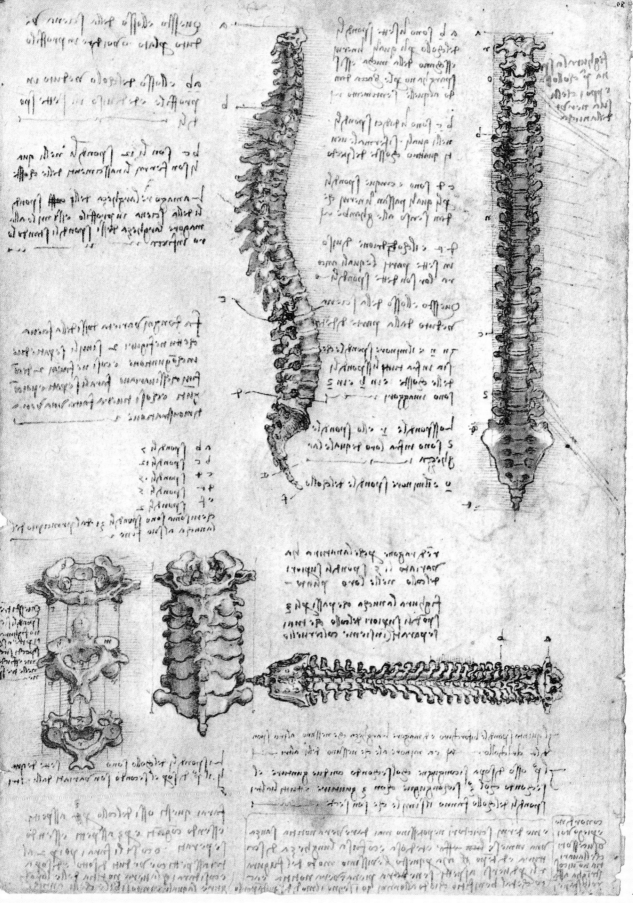

2

1.-5. Drawings
of mechanisms
"paginated"
for printing
Madrid Ms I
f. 2 r, f. 30 r, f. 43 r,
f. 50 r, f. 99 r
c. 1495-1497

6. Drawing
of hammer
winches
"paginated"
for printing
Madrid Ms I
f. 92 v
c. 1495-1497

details of an anatomical drawing. This is why in the draft printing of the *Libro di pittura*, carried forward by his pupils after his death, the illustrations planned by Leonardo himself are limited to diagrams and small schematic figures easily reproducible by xylography, and, moreover, at low cost.

And the machines? These too, if not designed to be built or offered to possible customers, could be drawn with the idea of publicizing them through printing. Some hints of this can be found in Leonardo's manuscripts, as when he insists that a machine should be represented in its basic elements, without its shell, so that its operation can be immediately understood. In the first of the Madrid manuscripts he states, in about 1497: «All such instruments will generally be presented without their armatures or other structures that might hinder the view of those who will study them».

Machines that are to be studied, then. All of the text on that page seems in fact to foreshadow the technological repertoires of the great French encyclopedias, from Belidor's hydraulic encyclopedia to Diderot's universal one. It is thus unsurprising that he concludes by describing how extremely heavy objects can be salvaged from the seabed through a method which has been applied with spectacular results in the nautical technology of our own times:

«We shall describe how air can be forced under water to lift very heavy weights, that is, how to fill skins with air once they are secured to weights at the bottom of the water».

And it is even less surprising that in books printed in France and Germany, but also in Italy, from the late 16th century on, Leonardo's machines appear again and again, at times with such identical details as to leave no doubt of their origin.

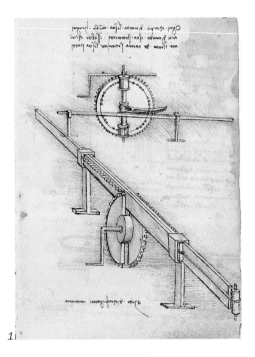

1

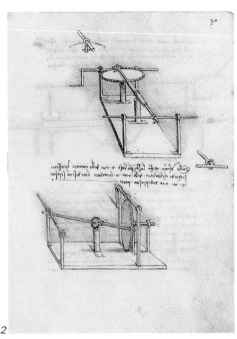

2

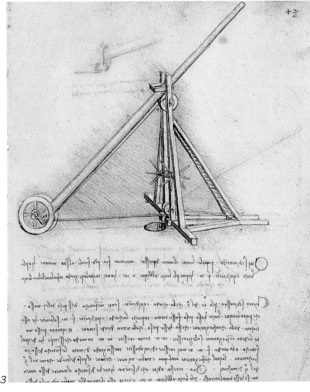

3

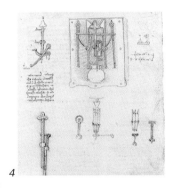

4

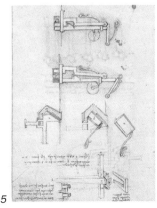

5

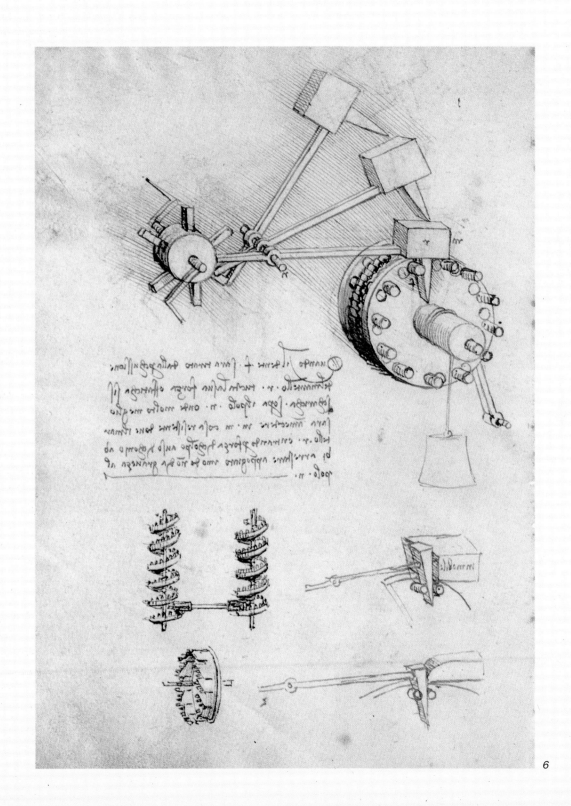

1.-5. Drawings
of weapons,
war machines
and military
architecture from
the Codex
Atlanticus copied
by F. François
and L. Ferrario
(Milan 1841)

frontispiece, plates
X, XII, XIV, XXXV:
first example
of systematic
reproduction
of a "corpus" of
technological
drawings by
Leonardo

1

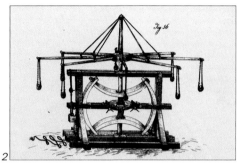

3

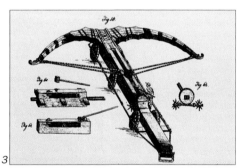

5

2

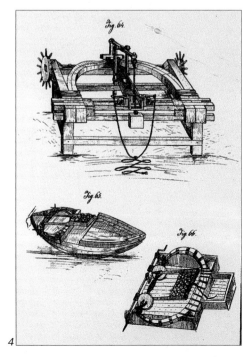

4

CREATION AND BENEFITS

Leonardo spent the last three years of his life in France, as the guest of King Francis I in the Castle of Clos-Lucé near Amboise, where in 1517, two years before his death, he was visited by Cardinal Louis d'Aragon.

To the illustrious prelate and his entourage Leonardo showed paintings, drawings, and above all manuscripts: «an infinite number of volumes», wrote the Cardinal's secretary in his *Diary*, «and all in the vulgar tongue, which would be most profitable and enjoyable should they ever come to light». Perhaps Leonardo himself had spoken to his guests of these writings as works he intended to publish, although realizing that this was now to be a task for posterity.

The work of compiling had become for him, more than ever, a daily habit, no longer a burden. Nothing could interfere with the laborious process of transcribing, elaborating, reviewing his own notes with patience, determination and even humility, vigilant in the awareness that his work could bring benefits that must not be lost: «Look over all these cases tomorrow and copy them, and then cross the original through and leave them in Florence, so that, if you should lose those that you take along, the invention will not be lost». These words were written in about 1508, at the time when the Codex Hammer was compiled.

In the end, then, he was again a man absorbed by the fervor and anxiety of works that must be completed even when physical strength was ebbing, even when he could have rested on his laurels.

Leonardo, already an old man, left Italy. It was not to find refuge in the welcoming protection of a King of France, but to contribute to the creation of a future that for him had already begun.

In an article on Leonardo's graphic arts published in London in 1971, Ladislao Reti pointed out an invention of Leonardo's that was an extraordinary forerunner of the printing method introduced by William Blake in the late 18th century for the simultaneous reproduction of texts and drawings. The invention of the printing press with movable characters dates back to the mid-15th century, just at the time of Leonardo's birth.

But in the second of the manuscripts found in Madrid, he himself proposes a printing method which, at substantially lower cost, would facilitate the immediate diffusion of his writings and drawings.

This was a new kind of relief etching on metal which is described on f. 119 r of the Madrid Manuscript II as follows:

«Of casting this work in print. Coat the iron plate with white lead and eggs and then write on it left-handed, scratching the ground. This done, you shall cover everything with a coat of varnish, that is, a varnish containing giallolino or minium. Once dry, leave the plate to soak, and the ground of the letters, written on the white lead and eggs, will be removed together with the minium. As the minium is frangible, it will break away leaving the letters adhering to the copper plate.

LEONARDO LIKE BLAKE

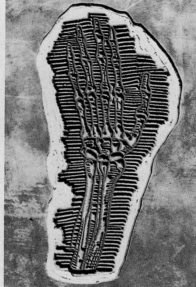

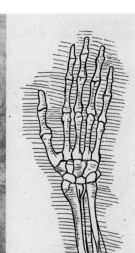

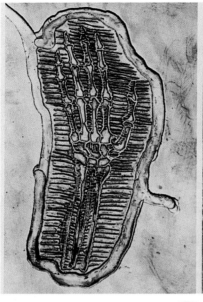

After this, hollow out the ground in your own way and the letters will stay in relief on a low ground. You may also blend minium with hard resin and apply it warm, as mentioned before, and it will be more frangible. In order to see the letters more clearly, stain the plate with fumes of sulphur which will incorporate itself with the copper».

Following these instructions, an artist of our own times, Attilio Rossi, has reproduced the detail of a hand from a folio of anatomical studies drawn by Leonardo in 1510, now at Windsor, no. 19009 v. It would be interesting to repeat the experiment including Leonardo's writing as well which, according to his instructions, would appear normally, no longer in mirror image.

Above, Attilio Rossi, print of anatomical drawing by Leonardo executed by the method described in Madrid Ms II, f. 119 r, c. 1504
Near left, system of physiotypic printing, CA f. 197 v, c. 1508-1510
Far left, William Blake, illustration for America: A Prophecy, *1793, plate 10 («Orc in the fires of energy»)*

CHRONOLOGY

1452

Leonardo is born at Vinci on April 15, the natural son of the notary Ser Piero di Antonio da Vinci.

At Arezzo, in the Church of San Francesco, Piero della Francesca begins the cycle of frescoes known as the *Legend of the True Cross*.

1454

The Peace of Lodi inaugurates a period of political stability in Italy.

1469

Leonardo presumably enters Verrocchio's workshop in this year.

1472

He is enrolled in the painters' association, the Compagnia di San Luca. His first works start from this date: costumes and sets for festivals and jousts, a cartoon for a tapestry (lost) and the paintings of uncertain dating.

1473

He dates (August 5) the drawing of the *Landscape of the Val d'Arno* (Florence, The Uffizi).

1476

Accused of sodomy along with other persons, he is acquitted.

In Milan Galeazzo Maria Sforza is assassinated in a plot. His son Gian Galeazzo succeeds him; the city is governed by Simonetta.

1478

Leonardo is commissioned to paint the altarpiece for the Chapel of San Bernardo in Palazzo della Signoria. In this same year he states that he has completed two paintings of the Virgin, one of which is now identified as the *Madonna Benois*.

The Pazzi Conspiracy, fomented by Pope Sixtus IV, fails. Giuliano de' Medici dies, but the authority of his brother Lorenzo the Magnificent is reinforced.

1480

According to the "Anonimo Gaddiano", Leonardo works for Lorenzo de' Medici.

Ludovico Sforza kills Simonetta, imprisons his nephew and illicitly becomes the lord of Milan.

1481

Contract for the *Adoration of the Kings*.

1482

Leonardo moves to Milan leaving the *Adoration of the Kings* unfinished.

1483

In Milan Leonardo stipulates the contract for the *Virgin of the Rocks* in collaboration with Evangelista and Ambrogio De Predis.

Raphael is born in Urbino.

1487

Payment for projects for the lantern on the Milan Cathedral.

1488

Verrocchio dies in Venice, where he was completing the equestrian monument to Colleoni. Bramante is in Pavia as consultant for designing the Cathedral.

1489

Leonardo designs sets for the festivities celebrating the wedding of Gian Galeazzo Sforza and Isabella d'Aragon. In this same year he begins preparations for the colossal equestrian statue in honor of Francesco Sforza.

1491

Giangiacomo Caprotti da Oreno, known as "Salai", enters Leonardo's service. The nickname "Salai", which means "devil", derives from the boy's unruly character.

1492

For the wedding of Ludovico il Moro and Beatrice d'Este, Leonardo designs the costumes for the parade of Scythians and Tartars.

In Florence Lorenzo de' Medici dies. The system of alliances sanctioned by the Peace of Lodi begins to break up.

1494

Land reclamation work on one of the Duke's estates near Vigevano.

The King of France Charles VIII, allying himself with Ludovico il Moro, invades Italy to claim his right to the Kingdom of Naples.

1495

Leonardo begins the *Last Supper* and the decoration of rooms in the Castello Sforzesco. The artist's name is mentioned as Ducal Engineer.

1497

The Duke of Milan urges the artist to finish the *Last Supper*, which is probably completed by the end of the year.

1498

Leonardo completes the decoration of the Sala delle Asse in the Castello Sforzesco.

Pollaiolo dies in Rome, where he has designed the tombs of Sixtus IV and Innocent VIII. Michelangelo is commissioned to sculpt the *Pietà* in St. Peter's. In Florence Savonarola is burned at the stake.

1499

Leonardo leaves Milan in the company of Luca Pacioli. Stops first at Vaprio to visit the Melzi family, then leaves for Venice passing through Mantua, where he draws two portraits of Isabella d'Este.

Luca Signorelli begins the frescoes in the Chapel of San Brizio in the Orvieto Cathedral. Milan is occupied by the King of France, Louis XII.

1500

Leonardo arrives in Venice in March. Returns to Florence where he resides in the Monastery of the Servite Brothers in the Santissima Annunziata.

In Florence, Piero di Cosimo paints the *Stories of Primitive Humanity*.

1502

Leonardo enters the service of Cesare Borgia as architect and general engineer, following him on his military campaigns through Romagna.

In Rome, Bramante begins the Tempietto di San Pietro in Montorio and the Belvedere Courtyard.

1503

Leonardo returns to Florence where, according to Vasari, he paints the *Mona Lisa*. Devises projects for deviating the course of the Arno River during the siege of Pisa. Commissioned by the Signoria to paint the *Battle of Anghiari*.

1504

Continues to work on the *Battle of Anghiari*. Is called upon to participate in the commission that will decide where to place Michelangelo's *David*. First studies for the *Leda and the Swan*.

Michelangelo completes the *David* commissioned from him three years before by the Republic of Florence. Raphael paints the *Marriage of the Virgin*; then moves to Florence, where he is profoundly influenced by Leonardo's work.

1506

Leonardo leaves Florence for Milan, planning to return within three months. The stay in Milan extends beyond this time.

1508

Leonardo is in Florence, then returns to Milan.

In Rome, Michelangelo commits himself to frescoing the ceiling of the Sistine Chapel. In Venice, Giorgione and Titian fresco the Fondaco dei Tedeschi.

1509

Geological studies on the valleys of Lombardy.

Raphael is in Rome, where he begins decorating the *Stanze*.

1510

Studies on anatomy with Marcantonio della Torre at the University of Pavia.

1512

Michelangelo completes the frescoes on the ceiling of the Sistine Chapel. The Sforza return to Milan.

1513

Leonardo leaves Milan for Rome, where he lives in the Vatican Belvedere under the protection of Giuliano de' Medici. Remains in this city for three years, engaged in mathematical and scientific studies.

Pope Julius II dies. He is succeeded by Giovanni de' Medici under the name of Leo X. In Florence, Andrea del Sarto begins the cycle of frescoes *Stories of the Virgin*. In Milan, Cesare da Sesto with his *Baptism of Christ* achieves a synthesis of the style of Leonardo and that of Raphael.

1514

Projects for draining the Pontine swamps and for the port of Civitavecchia.

In Rome Bramante dies. Raphael succeeds him as architect of the Fabric of St. Peter's.

1515

Francis I becomes King of France. With the victory of Marignano he reconquers Milan. Raphael works on the cartoons for the tapestries in the Sistine Chapel.

1516

Charles of Hapsburg becomes King of Spain.

1517

Leonardo moves to Amboise, to the court of Francis I, King of France. In mid-January he visits Romorantin with the King to plan a new royal residence and a system of canals in the region of Sologne.

In Rome, Raphael and his assistants paint the "Logge" in the Vatican and the Loggia of Psyche in the Villa Farnesina.

1518

Leonardo participates in the festivities for the baptism of the Dauphin and for the wedding of Lorenzo de' Medici to the King's niece.

1519

On April 23 Leonardo writes his will. The executor is his friend the painter Francesco Melzi. He dies on May 2. In the burial certificate, dated August 12, he is described as a «noble Milanese, first painter and engineer and architect to the King, State Mechanical Engineer».

Charles V of Hapsburg is elected Emperor of the Holy Roman Empire. Open conflict breaks out between France and the Empire. In Parma, Correggio paints the Badessa's Chamber in the Convent of San Paolo.

INDEX

PHOTOGRAPHS
Archivio Giunti
The publisher is well prepared to meet all copyright obligations
pertainy to those photographs the sources of which could not be ascertained